WARRIOR 172

APACHE WARRIOR 1860–86

ROBERT N. WATT

ILLUSTRATED BY ADAM HOOK

Series editor Marcus Cowper

First published in Great Britain in 2014 by Osprey Publishing,
PO Box 883, Oxford, OX1 9PL, UK
PO Box 3985, New York, NY 10185-3985, USA
E-mail: info@ospreypublishing.com

A CIP catalogue record for this book is available from the British Library.

ISBN: 978 1 4728 0352 8
E-book ISBN: 978 1 4728 0354 2
PDF ISBN: 978 1 4728 0353 5

Editorial by Ilios Publishing Ltd, Oxford, UK (www.iliospublishing.com)
Index by Mark Swift
Typeset in Myriad Pro and Sabon
Artwork by Adam Hook
Originated by PDQ Media, UK
Printed in China through Worldprint Ltd.

14 15 16 17 18 10 9 8 7 6 5 4 3 2 1

www.ospreypublishing.com

ACKNOWLEDGEMENTS

The author would like to thank the following for their help
and encouragement:

Catherine Edwards, Willy Dobak, Dan Aranda, Emilio Tapia, Lynda Sanchez,
Deni Seymour, Berndt Kuhn, Ed Sweeney, Bill Cavaliere, Eric and Kathy
Fuller, Spike Flanders, Frank Brito, Mary Williams, Karl Laumbach, Toni Sudar
Laumbach, Ron Burkett, James Irby, Allan Radbourne, Robert Wooster,
Durwood Ball, Bruce Dinges, Diana Hadley, Bob Roland, James Rees,
Richard North, Craig Springer, Jay Van Orden, Richard Wakefield, Frank
Parrish, Stephen Lekson, Anthony Romero, Joe Arcure, Kathy Klump, Alan
Ferg, Bernd Brand, Laraine Daly Jones, J.R. Absher, Kira Watt, Lincoln County
Historical Society, Arizona Historical Society (AHS), Geronimo Springs
Museum, Deming Luna County Museum, Hillsboro Historical Society,
Chiricahua Regional Museum.

ARTIST'S NOTE

Readers may care to note that the original paintings from which the colour
plates in this book were prepared are available for private sale. The
Publishers retain all reproduction copyright whatsoever. All enquiries
should be addressed to:

Scorpio, 158 Mill Road, Hailsham, East Sussex BN27 2SH, UK
scorpiopaintings@btinternet.com

The Publishers regret that they can enter into no correspondence upon
this matter.

Front cover:

Four Chiricahua Apache warriors photographed by C. S. Fly of Tombstone
during General Crook's conference with Geronimo in Canon De Los Embudos,
March, 1886. From left to right Yanozha, Chappo (son of Geronimo),
Yahe-chul (also known as Fun) and Geronimo. Yahe-chul was a particularly
courageous fighter winning particular distinction in a savage battle with
Mexican troops in 1882. (See p. 58) They are armed, again from left to right,
two Winchester repeating rifles, a Springfield carbine and a Springfield rifle.
(US Army Heritage and Education Center)

CONTENTS

APACHE WARRIOR 1860–86

Mangus, son of the great Mangas Coloradas, was the last leader to surrender to the US authorities in 1886. His role in the late 1870s and early 1880s is obscure but some US Army correspondence portrays him as leading a significant following among the Warm Springs Apaches who survived Tres Castillos in 1880. The US civil authorities clearly assumed him to be closely associated with Victorio in 1880, as his arrest warrant shows. He appears to have a Springfield carbine laid across his lap. While the popular image of the Chiricahua Apache warrior armed with a Winchester repeating rifle is not inaccurate, single-shot, breech-loading rifles/carbines of Springfield or Remington manufacture were equally popular and archaeological evidence strongly suggests that the Apaches appreciated the longer effective range of such weapons. (Photo courtesy of National Archaeological Archives, Smithsonian)

INTRODUCTION

Any mention of the Chiricahua Apache warrior evokes the idea of endurance, the image of a man who is elusively cunning, ferocious and cruel. Such portrayals of warriors were prevalent during the Apache Wars of the 1860s to the 1880s and are, to some extent, still believed today. General George Crook admired Apache warriors as "Human Tigers," yet other members of the US Army took a very different view. For example, Lt. Charles P. Elliott[1] stated that:

The Apache Indian is as perfect a savage as this country has ever produced, and it is impossible to conceive of greater cruelty and less natural affection in any creature that walks on two legs. The fiendish cruelties committed by them when on the warpath give one a creepy feeling while among them, and when a son brings in his father's head on which a reward had been placed, not because he had trouble with him, but because he happened to know where he was in hiding and wanted the reward, it makes one doubt whether they are human.

The truth of the matter is that most opponents of the Chiricahua Apaches simply did not understand their culture and hence their approach to warfare.

---

[1] Elliott was an officer in the 4th Cavalry from 1883 until his retirement in 1898. He was detached from the 4th Cavalry soon after his arrival at Fort Lowell in 1883 to serve as a provost officer on the San Carlos Reservation. As such, he would have had very close contact with Apache warriors during the last phase of the Apache Wars. However, he does not seem to have felt the need to familiarize himself with Apache culture. See Charles P. Elliott, 'An Indian Reservation Under General George Crook', *Military Affairs*, Vol. 12, Issue 2 (Summer 1948), pp. 91–102.

THE PRESIDENT of the UNITED STATES of AMERICA

To The United States Marshal for the District of New Mexico, Greeting:

You ARE HEREBY COMMANDED to arrest and take the body of _Mangus_ _(An Indian)_ .... and him safely keep, so that you have him before the UNITED STATES DISTRICT COURT, within and for the Third Judicial District of New Mexico, at their next term, to be begun and held in the County of Doña Ana, at the Court House in said County, on the _First_ Monday of _September_ A. D. 188_0_ to answer to the charge of _Stealing Horses, Mules and Pistols_ ....

Hereof fail not, and have you then and there this writ.

WITNESS the Hon WARREN BRISTOL, Associate Justice of the Supreme Court of said Territory, and Judge of the Third Judicial District Court, and the seal of said Court, this _29th_ day of _March_ A. D. 188_0_

George R. Bowman Clerk.

Mangus' arrest warrant for "Stealing Horses, Mules and Pistols" issued on March 29, 1880. On the reverse it is endorsed: "The United States Viz/Vs Victorio et al. Warrant. I certify that after diligent search, I am unable to find the Indian named 'Mangus' in my District so that I may have him before this Court as I am within commanded. John Sherman for United States Marshal." One suspects that while the search may have been diligent, John Sherman was probably lucky not to have found or been found by Mangus. (Author's photo – courtesy of access given by the Parrish Collection)

Thus even sympathetic opponents gave the Apache warriors credit for being very effective guerrilla fighters while at the same time implying that they were not quite human as understood by civilized society. Chiricahua warriors were depicted as superhuman and any sign of success against the USA was seen as being due to inherent traits rather than because they belonged to a culture that, on their own territory, was equal or even superior to that of their American opponents. This biological explanation of the success of the Chiricahua Apache also implied that there was no evolutionary element driving their success. In other words, this view failed to realize that part of the effectiveness of Chiricahua Apache resistance was that a key element of their continued survival was their ability to evolve in response to new opponents or tactical and technological changes among existing enemies.

What this book will seek to establish is that the Chiricahua warrior's approach to survival was carefully calculated and shaped by years of preparation. It was adaptable enough to allow individuals to develop and disseminate new information concerning the strengths and weaknesses of their enemies in the light of their ongoing contact with their foes. The expertise required to survive in their environment was beyond mere inherited ability, but the result of clear thinking by very intelligent and adaptive human beings. The reason they had to become so successful as raiders and hunters was their refusal to bow to colonization: first Spanish, then Mexican and finally American efforts to settle in, and economically exploit, Apacheria. If the Apaches were quite ruthless opponents, it was because their foes were just as brutal when encountering opposition whilst, in their eyes, bringing light to darkest Apacheria. A lack of numbers forced the Apaches to focus their abilities upon becoming adept guerrilla fighters. A study by Lekson shows that from the very start of contact with colonization, the Chihenne Apache, who relied upon being able to harvest food at certain locations at certain times

The lower slopes of the San Mateo Mountains in New Mexico looking approximately southwards towards the settlement of Canada Alamosa, the inhabitants of which maintained good trading relations with the Chihenne Apaches. In January 1880, approximately five companies of 9th Cavalry (Buffalo Soldiers) and a company of Apache scouts, commanded by Major Albert P. Morrow, pursued about 60 well-armed and well-mounted Apaches up this valley. Morrow recorded that for almost five days he engaged in an exhausting pursuit, punctuated by several inconclusive firefights with the Apaches, through this type of terrain. (Author's Photo)

of the year, found their subsistence range was increasingly constricted. This encouraged the Chihenne to increase their raiding activities and thus also increase the instances of conflict between them and their would-be colonizers.

Organization of Chiricahua Apache society

The organization of Chiricahua Apache society is a bit of an anthropological minefield, as Chiricahua Apache society was a complex network of both hostile and friendly family and friendship links. The easiest way to understand how they fitted together is to remember that the US Army of the time applied the term 'Chiricahua' generally to a number of related groups of Apaches. As such, what have been termed the Central (Chokonen), Eastern (Chihenne) and Southern (Nehdni) Chiricahua Apaches will be the focus of our study. This can also be extended to the Bedonkohe Apaches who lived to the east of the Chihenne and to the north of the Chokonen Apaches. To see these groups as clearly distinct is convenient but not particularly accurate. For example, Geronimo was born a Bedonkohe but married into the Nehdni. Other Chiricahua Apaches married into the Western or Mescalero Apache and vice versa – the custom was that the man left to join his wife's family. Equally, while there may have been instances of alliances or conflicts between the Chiricahuas and other Apache groups, internal disputes could easily erupt into violence within, for example, the Chihennes. In 1873 Chihenne leaders Loco and Nana dealt with a leadership challenge by the four sons of the late Chihenne leader Cuchillo Negro by using violence. Two of the four sons of Cuchillo Negro were killed in a point-blank gun battle and a third was badly wounded. Nevertheless, two leaders who were widely believed to dislike each other, Victorio (Chihenne) and Juh (Nehdni), were capable of putting aside their differences to briefly ally against a common enemy in October and November 1879. In doing so, they inflicted a sharp defeat upon pursuing US forces in northern Mexico.

The hazards of relaxing one's guard can be seen in this memorial to four soldiers killed by Apaches in 1866. This monument can still be seen in the graveyard at Fort Cummings. The heavily weathered inscription reads: "SACRED TO THE MEMORY OF THOS RONAN AGED 45 LS HUNTER AGED 33 CHAS DEVLIN AGED 28 THOS DALY AGED 28 LATE PRIVATES OF CO G 1ST VETERAN INFANTRY CAL. VOLS. KILLED BY APACHES AT OAK GROVE NM JAN 17 1866" (Author's photo)

CHRONOLOGY

December 1860	An unprovoked attack on an Apache village by a party of miners incites Mangas Coloradas to go to war with the Americans.
February 1861	A false accusation of raiding and kidnapping provokes Cochise into open warfare with the USA. He and Mangas Coloradas join forces to fight the Americans.
1861–62	With the outbreak of the Civil War the few troops based in Arizona depart and those citizens left in the territory find themselves besieged by the infuriated Apaches.
1862	As part of an effort to drive Confederate forces out of Arizona and New Mexico, General Carleton advances east at the head of volunteer Union troops raised in California. The advance guard is ambushed in Apache Pass by a large group of Apache warriors led by Cochise and Mangas Coloradas. The deployment of two mountain howitzers wins the day for the Californians.
1862–71	A prolonged guerrilla war of attrition against the USA is undertaken by the Chiricahua Apaches led by Cochise and Mangas Coloradas. The latter was taken prisoner under a flag of truce and "shot while trying to escape" in January 1863, but Cochise continued the fight. Neither side gained the upper hand. However, throughout this period US and Mexican forces both inflicted steady casualties upon the Chiricahua Apaches, which ultimately proved unsustainable. By 1871, Cochise was willing to consider peace overtures.
June 1871	Crook arrives to take command of US troops in Arizona. His use of Apache scouts and mule trains would prove instrumental in the fight against the Apaches.
September–October 1872	General O. O. Howard concludes a peace treaty with Cochise and the latter agrees to settle on a reservation based around the Dragoon and Chiricahua Mountains. This audacious act brings an end to Cochise's 11-year war with the USA. It also prevented Crook targeting the Chiricahua Apaches as part of his up-coming offensive against the Apaches in Arizona.
1876	The Chiricahua reservation based around Fort Bowie is closed under the auspices of the Dept. of the Interior, which instituted a new policy to concentrate all Apaches on one reservation. This policy is probably responsible for the Apache Wars of 1877–86. Juh, leader of the Nehdni/Southern Chiricahuas, refuses to accept this closure and leads his followers back into Mexico. He is accompanied by Geronimo, widely regarded as Juh's right-hand man. Most of the Chokonen/Central Chiricahuas under the leadership of Taza and Naiche accept the move to San Carlos after gunning down the two leading Chokonen opponents (Eskinya and Pionsenay) to the closure.

1877–79	The concentration policy gathers momentum as the Warm Springs Apache reservation at Ojo Caliente, New Mexico, is closed and the Apaches led by Victorio, Loco and Nana are transferred to San Carlos in May 1877. They quickly voice opposition to the move and leave the reservation in September 1877. Between October 1877 and August 1879, Victorio and Nana fought for a return to Ojo Caliente while Loco chose to return to the reservation and pursue the same goal peacefully. In fact, it is probable that there were individuals and small groups of Chiricahua Apaches who never accepted the reservation system also at large during the period 1872–86. These individuals would have continued raiding independently and on occasion in alliance with leaders such as Victorio, Nana, Juh, and Geronimo.
	During the closure of Ojo Caliente Geronimo, who had been raiding on both sides of the border and periodically taking refuge at Ojo Caliente, is arrested and transported to San Carlos in chains. Geronimo leaves the reservation in 1878 and rejoins Juh in Mexico.
1879–80	Having caused minimal casualties in the USA between 1877 and 1879, Victorio loses patience and wages an all-out war against the USA and Mexico. From September 1879 to May 1880 he outwits and defeats every force sent against him. His warriors inflict heavy casualties upon the citizens and soldiers of both countries. He is gradually worn down by a defeat at the hands of Apache scouts in May 1880 and by being outmaneuvered by the 10th Cavalry in Western Texas during July and August 1880. On October 14/15, 1880, Victorio is finally trapped and killed at Tres Castillos by Mexican state troops.
	Juh, having briefly allied with Victorio in 1879, had negotiated a return to San Carlos in January 1880 after sustaining a stinging defeat at the hands of Mexican troops. He was accompanied by Geronimo.
July–August 1881	Nana, Victorio's successor, having regrouped the survivors of Tres Castillos, launches a legendary raid into New Mexico. Aged around 75, he led his raiders approximately 1,500 miles in six weeks and held off or defeated at least seven US Army detachments and inflicted heavy casualties among the ranching and mining communities in southern New Mexico.
September 1881	Juh, Naiche, Geronimo and many Chiricahua Apaches flee the San Carlos Reservation, having become alarmed at the level of army activity in the aftermath of a revolt by Western Apaches, who had been provoked by their poor treatment on their reservations. After a couple of skirmishes with pursuing US Forces at K-H Butte and down the eastern edge of the Dragoon Mountains, the

	Chiricahua Apaches take refuge in the Sierra Madre. They soon join forces with Nana and his followers recently returned to Mexico from their raid into New Mexico.
April 1882	The Sierra Madre Apaches arrive at the San Carlos reservation and force Loco and his Chihenne Apaches to return with them to Mexico. They hold off the 4th Cavalry in a rearguard action at Horseshoe Canyon in Arizona. They are then surprised by a force of 6th Cavalry and Apache scouts near the Sierra Enmedio in Mexico, but after the initial surprise manage to hold off their attackers. On fleeing further south into Mexico, they are ambushed by Mexican troops who inflict catastrophic losses on the Chiricahuas. Of the 400 Apaches who left the reservation over 100 are killed before they reach the Sierra Madre.
May–June 1883	General Crook, with a force mainly made up of Western Apache scouts, penetrates the Chiricahua strongholds in the Sierra Madre Mountains in Mexico and persuades the Apaches to surrender.
February 1884	Geronimo becomes the last of the Chiricahua Apaches to arrive from Mexico after the peace agreement with General Crook arranged during the Sierra Madre expedition of 1883.
May 1885	Geronimo, Naiche, Mangus, Nana, Chihuahua, and Ulzana flee the San Carlos reservation.
November–December 1885	Chihuahua's brother, Ulzana, leads a small party of warriors into the USA and cause widespread disruption before returning to Mexico.
March 1886	General Crook meets with the Apaches at Canon de los Embudos and agrees to their surrender. Geronimo and Naiche then flee. Nana, Chihuahua, Ulzana and their followers surrender and are sent back to the USA. Crook resigns and is replaced by Nelson A. Miles. The Chiricahua Apaches who surrender and those who remained on the reservation are deported to Florida.Mangus had separated from the rest of the Apaches and did not take part in the negotiations.
September–October 1886	Geronimo surrenders in Skeleton Canyon. He and his followers are deported to Florida along with those Chiricahua Apaches who served as scouts. A small group led by Mangus returns to the USA and surrenders in mid-October; it is also deported to Florida.

BELIEF AND BELONGING

The Chiricahua Apaches followed a radical version of a principle of warfare common to all American Indians, that of sustaining the minimum of loss for the maximum damage inflicted on the enemy, be that through plunder acquired and/or casualties inflicted. Unlike professional opponents such as those serving in the US Army at the time, the loss of a warrior's life could have a direct and extreme economic effect, not just on his dependents but on the community as a whole. The man's family would become more dependent upon other warriors and their families in their struggle for survival, whereas the loss of a few enlisted men to Apache ambush would have little knock-on effect on US industrial society.

The Chiricahuas made this principle a lynchpin of their definition of success or failure in raiding or warfare. A leader who was seen to have lost followers by taking unnecessary risks would soon lose his following. For example, if during a raid the Apaches had taken many horses but lost a warrior due to the leader taking what was judged to be unnecessary risks, then his standing as a leader would soon fall as his followers sought other more successful leadership.

Effectively, Chiricahua Apaches were encouraged to conduct a thorough risk assessment of their intended actions in order to absolutely minimize the losses taken in warfare. Potential targets could be quietly monitored for days before undertaking an attack was even considered. The principle of "if there is doubt there is no doubt" was a key element of the risk analysis. In other words, if an Apache leader remained unsure as to the results of his intended action it would not reflect badly upon his status among his following if he chose not to attack. As we shall see, leadership was a key position for a Chiricahua warrior, as it bore a great deal of responsibility for the well-being of his followers. The art of persuasion was a key element of the decision to attack, or not, and would have been discussed with his warriors.

Nevertheless, while risk analysis may have minimized the dangers involved, it could not guarantee that there would be absolutely no risk at all. An unforeseen variable could always intervene and Chiricahua Apaches had to be able to react to these factors as quickly as possible. For example, on January 23, 1881, Chihenne Apaches, probably led by Nana, ambushed and pinned down seven civilians near Palomas in New Mexico until their siege was broken by a small detachment of the 9th Cavalry led by Sergeant Madison Ingoman[2]:

> The Regimental Commander takes great pleasure in announcing the gallant conduct and excellent judgement of Sergeant Madison Ingoman, Company D, 9th Cavalry, in two affairs with hostile Indians. On the 23rd of January, 1881, when in command of six men of Company D, 9th Cavalry, escorting a train of ten wagons en route to Ojo Caliente, New Mexico, at the sound of sharp firing, he corralled [sic] his train, and leaving it to be guarded by the teamsters, moved quickly in the direction of the firing, and found seven citizens defending themselves in a ravine against twenty-five Indians. He at once charged the Indians, routing them. On the 25th of January, 1881, while escorting the same

---

[2] The original citation for gallantry names Madison Ingoman but other sources name him as Daniel Ingoman.

train through the Canon of Canada Alamosa, the train was attacked by fifteen Indians; parking the train and preparing to defend it, it was apparent that the animals would soon be killed from the plunging fire of the Indians from the heights; he at once charged them on foot, the ground being impracticable for horses, and routed them, losing one man killed in the assault. He then skilfully covered and conducted the train eight miles to the out-post of Ojo Caliente, after the Indians had received an increase to their first party.

Army & Navy Journal, Volume 18, February 26, 1881, p. 608

In launching his attack to relieve the trapped civilians, Ingoman effectively forced the leader of the group of 25 Apaches to make an immediate calculation of the risk taken in standing their ground against this unexpected assault. By charging in with six men, Sgt. Ingoman was doing something no Apache leader would contemplate. The sudden arrival of a small detachment of Buffalo Soldiers might herald the approach of a larger force. The safest option for the Apaches was to abort their attack and review the situation from a safe distance as there was nothing to be gained by risking unnecessary fatalities. The Apaches, when realizing the small size of Ingoman's detachment, clearly thought that the numbers were in their favor. Realizing the train's destination, they were able to pick an ideal spot for an ambush a couple of days later.

The Apaches were almost certainly Chihenne, whose homeland centered around the hot springs at Ojo Caliente, and they would have known the surrounding countryside intimately. However, even when they had chosen the ground and had their opponents exactly where they wanted them, Sergeant Ingoman again did something that no Apache leader would have done – he charged a superior number of enemies who were well protected by the terrain. Once again the Apache leader was forced to make an immediate risk analysis and probably decided that the risk of taking fatalities was too great for the possible rewards, and again withdrew.

Reading the report carefully, one suspects that, by targeting the draft animals and cavalry mounts, the Apaches were trying to force a withdrawal, which would allow them to ransack the wagons undisturbed. While they shot and killed one of the men from the 9th Cavalry during Ingoman's charge, they did not consider standing their ground was worth the risk of taking fatalities. The Apaches would probably not have known the exact content of the wagons, and the loss of a couple of men for the chance that there may have been ammunition among the loads was not worth the risk. An Apache leader would not contemplate risking fatalities for unknown rewards, especially as these same Apaches had earlier found out that wagon loads could be a bit of a lottery. On January 14, 1881, they destroyed a wagon and stagecoach in the Goodsight Mountains, about 60 miles to the south, and five people were killed. The wagon contained a load of fish, which, according to Opler, many Apaches considered taboo as a food staple.[3]

Canada Alamosa Canyon. This is the type of terrain chosen by the Apaches to ambush Sergeant Ingoman's detachment as it made its way to Ojo Caliente on 25 January 1881. One can see how the Chiricahuas would have been able to occupy well-protected positions not only high above but also close to the canyon floor. This would give them the best chance to fulfi their ethos of maximum damage to their enemies with minimum damage to themselves. (Author's photo)

---

[3] Opler interviewed his subjects in the 1930s and noted that this dislike of fish appeared to be more prevalent among the older generation of Chiricahua Apaches.

This photo shows an Apache scout from 1888 dressed in traditional garb and armed with traditional weaponry. His hairstyle is unusual and may reflect European influence. However, of more interest are the crosses worn round his neck. They might have reflected Christian influence. However, early Jesuits noticed the Apache use of cross iconography and had mistaken them for a lost Christian tribe when in fact the cross reflected the four sacred directions and thus had nothing to do with Christianity. (Photo courtesy of National Archaeological Archives, Smithsonian)

Developmental psychology helps us to understand why the Apaches were so adept at survival by hunting and raiding. Jean Piaget's concept of "formal operations" states that formal operational thinking marks the most advanced level of thinking as the adolescent moves into adulthood and develops abstract reasoning. Some critics of Piaget argue that not all individuals attain this level of development, pointing out that many members of both literate and, particularly, non-literate cultures fail to reason at this level. One response to this argument is that many individuals only utilize formal operational thinking in specific situations, especially where they are dealing with matters that are essential to their continued survival. A study of pre-literate bushmen society by Tulkin and Konner (1973) discovered that bushman hunters, who appear to fail Piaget's tests (which are designed to demonstrate an ability to deploy formal operational thinking), do think at this level when hunting. Here the bushmen clearly demonstrate a systematic testing of inferences and hypotheses when tracking their prey, which are essential for their continued survival.

A   THE APACHE WARRIOR, EARLY 1860S

The Apache warrior of the early 1860s (**1**) was aware of the danger of cloth infections in wounds. Therefore, when raiding or going to war he would wear the minimum of clothing: a breechclout, worn narrow and short at the front and wider and longer to the rear; long Apache boots, which provided some protection from the spiny flora ubiquitous to Apacheria; and a headband. His primary weapon would be the bow and arrow (**2**) with the quiver (**3**) carried in one of two ways:

> When the Chiricahuas are on the march and are not using their arrows, they carry them so that the feathers come over the top of the right shoulder. When they are fighting, they reverse the bag so that the feathers come under the left armpit, and they can be snatched out of the quiver with the right hand. For a left-handed person it is just the opposite. Sometimes the quiver is carried over the chest so it will be more handy. (Opler, 1996, p.341.)

This particular warrior is carrying his quiver in the "march" position and is probably hunting game. Sometimes the lance, wielded two-handed on foot, would be used. The one illustrated (**4**) is held in the museum of the Arizona Historical Society. Captured or traded knives or broken sabres would be used to provide lance blades. This example is unusual in that most of the sabre blade has been incorporated into the lance. Normally, sabre blades would be broken and the upper part used as the lance blade. The blade would be shorter and straight if a knife was used. The flop-headed war club was also carried and a skilled warrior would make maximum use of the deadly impact of its slingshot effect (**5**). By the early 1860s, muskets were fairly common (**6**). The Springfield and Enfield rifled muskets would have been the most modern varieties in Apache hands at that time. However, one suspects that older trade muskets would have been more common. Much less common would have been the Sharps carbine and the Spencer and Henry repeating rifles.

This and the following three photographs are dated either 1886 or 1888 by the Smithsonian. However, British historian Allan Radbourne notes that these photos date to 1884 and are photographs of Chiricahua Apaches shortly after they arrived at San Carlos having surrendered to General Crook in the Sierra Madre Mountains in Mexico. This man is named Frijole and his body language is interesting; he is very relaxed with his Springfield carbine across his lap but his gaze into the camera is very alert. He is listed as being part of Nana's following. (Photo courtesy of National Archaeological Archives, Smithsonian)

Where the Apaches were concerned, they concentrated their formal operational thinking upon the key skills of hunting, gathering and raiding. As the activity of raiding could often lead into warfare, this too became the focus of their highest level of thinking.

If we return to the attack upon Sergeant Ingoman's detachment in Canada Alamosa Canyon on January 25, 1881, the Apaches, once they had had time to quietly look over their unexpected opponents of 23 January, had realized their small numbers. They had clearly judged that this new target was worth ambushing and, realizing where the detachment was bound, worked out exactly where they could be attacked. That the attack failed does not detract from the abstract thinking behind the ambush.

A more involved example would be the period between September 4 and 18, 1879, when Chihenne leader, Victorio, pinpointed a number of threats and dealt with them consecutively. On September 4, his warriors ambushed the horse herd belonging to Company E, 9th Cavalry, at Ojo Caliente, New Mexico. This was the only US Army unit actually stationed in the immediate vicinity of the hostile Apaches. The supply lines for Ojo Caliente were constantly harassed during this period, and, with the majority of its horses lost, the small garrison was effectively neutralized until replacement horses were delivered in December 1879. The September 4 attack attracted the general attention of three 9th Cavalry detachments that were in the field looking for Victorio. On September 10/11, Victorio's warriors struck the community of Jaralosa and McEvers Ranch. These attacks led to an armed posse of citizens, drawn from the large mining camp at Hillsboro, being ambushed just outside McEvers Ranch. This drew the above US Army detachments to that ranch and a fairly obvious trail was laid by the Apaches along the Rio Las Animas into the Black Range. Here the cavalry detachments were ambushed and the mauling they received forced them to withdraw to Fort Bayard. In the space of 15 days, the Chihennes had neutralized the immediate threats to their continued independence and they had clearly thought up this perfectly executed plan in advance.

Risk-analysis style of warfare was also demonstrated by the difference between Chiricahua Apache "raiding" and "warfare." For the Apaches, "raiding" was not intended to provoke conflict but to appropriate property from enemies, whereas the intention of "warfare" was to wreak vengeance for losses inflicted by enemies. This distinction makes a lot of sense when one appreciates the Chiricahua attitude towards risk. If the intent during a raid was only to take property, then the chances of sustaining fatalities were clearly reduced. However, this does not mean that warriors would not kill unwary travellers or sentries in order to take property, nor that pursuing

enemies might not catch up and kill or wound some Apaches, but the risk of such losses would be considerably reduced if the raiders did not seek battle. On the other hand, war was clearly associated with revenge. Long-time American Indian and Mexican communities would quickly come to realize, through trade contact with the Chiricahuas, that if they killed a raider they could expect some form of fatal retribution. This knowledge in itself might reduce Apache losses as their enemies might refrain from killing raiders even if they recovered their property.

The numbers involved in raiding were also small:

As few as five or six would be in the party. About ten is the most that would go. Usually, but not always, one who had power connected with war was along… Each man took a robe or two along. Each took along a little food in a bag tied to his belt. Often no food was taken along, and the men killed something to eat on the way. Water was brought in a little bag made of entrails, which was carried in the hand. One of the party would bring along a fire drill which was carried in the quiver… If they were discovered by the owners of the cattle, they would usually run away without fighting. (Opler, 1996, p.334.)

The raid was not seen as an occasion for pomp or ceremony as, along with hunting, it was an integral part of being an Apache providing for his family. However, should war be contemplated then a war dance was proposed by those who had suffered loss. If the leading men agreed that vengeance was required then this would go ahead, and the numbers volunteering would not be restricted as with raiding parties. The dance gave all those intending to confront the enemy a chance to declare their intentions to their audience, and the Apache believed that the dance would bring success and protect the warriors in the coming fight.

The use of an individual's name also had clear significance as, if during the dance, a man's name was called upon to volunteer, it was very unusual for him to decline as this would undermine not only his general social standing but also his self-esteem.

These three photographs are of two Chiricahua warriors: José, or Joe, and Petal (this no doubt being an Anglicized phonetic reproduction of the warrior's Apache name). José is listed as a 28-year-old member of Geronimo's following. Both men appear more tense and suspicious than Frijole but just as alert. Having recently returned to San Carlos they were probably still wary of possible treachery on the part of the US authorities. (Photos courtesy of National Archaeological Archives, Smithsonian)

The number four had clear religious significance for the Chiricahua Apaches. According to Opler's account of the war dance there were a number of variations, but his informants noted that four men might start the dance, or that the dancing would last four days, or that in praying the warrior might blow smoke to the four directions (east, south, west and north). As we shall see, these cultural beliefs reinforce the Apache emphasis upon success in raiding and warfare: "The men doing the dance did not shout. They just made a noise softly under their breath like, 'Wah! Wah!' You can't shout in a war dance or in war. The belief that has been handed down is that, if you shout in battle, many of you will be killed. Those along the sides shout though." (Opler, 1996, p.337.)

For the Chiricahua warrior, success in both raiding and battle depended upon stealth. Thus, a young Apache would be surrounded by stories and beliefs designed to produce an adult steeped in these values. Apache children, seeing the audience making a lot of noise but the warriors dancing making the minimum of noise, had the value of stealth reinforced.

Once we understand how the roles of raiding and warfare were key to the lives of the Chiricahuas, we can also see the source of their proficiency in guerrilla warfare. Apache warriors were the products of a culture that lauded formal operational thinking as it could be applied to hunting, gathering, raiding and warfare. They fought specifically to their own strengths, waging guerrilla warfare on their own terms and not allowing their opponents to set the agenda. This could only be developed by training children through adolescence to adulthood in a culture of survival, where promotion to leadership roles was by merit. It also fostered the promotion of individuals who could adapt to changes in their opponent's practices and technology in order to continue to survive.

TRAINING

James Kaywaykla, a young child in Victorio's following, recounted how a "creep and freeze" game twice saved his life when the Apaches were attacked by Mexican soldiers. When Victorio was trapped and killed at Tres Castillos during October 14/15, 1880, Kaywaykla was guided to safety by his mother, Gouyen, during the hours of darkness. One of the techniques they used to work their way through the Mexican lines was the "creep and freeze" method. This is probably based upon the idea that a combination of careful or minimal movement and patient waiting is an excellent means of avoiding visual detection. Opler notes that to point with the hand was seen as impolite and generally only done when angry.[4] Therefore, Apaches generally pointed with their noses or lips, rather than using the hands, to alert others to some object or danger. However, this etiquette around pointing could have had a particularly practical application during warfare, as to point with the nose or lips requires a minimum of movement. Much of Chiricahua Apache warfare techniques required concealment until the enemy was at the greatest possible disadvantage, and the more movement one makes when trying to remain hidden the more chance there is of being spotted prematurely.

I have traveled widely in Apacheria and find the flora and fauna to be of great interest. However, spotting a stationary mule deer in good cover is very

---

4   Opler, 1996, p.432.

difficult unless it moves. I have detected a deer which remained absolutely still but was vigorously flicking its ears to keep off the flies. On scanning the terrain I was attracted to the specific movement and then spotted the rest of the animal. The same principle would apply to experienced Mexican and US troops and most particularly to Apache scouts scanning the terrain for any sign of danger. If a concealed Chiricahua spotted something unexpected and needed to alert his compatriots, the alarm needed to be raised with the absolute minimum of movement and noise.

Obedience, trust, initiative and observation were key elements in the training of Apache children for their future lives as adult hunters, gatherers and raiders. Kaywaykla also recalled asking his grandmother how he could earn an Apache name rather than the Spanish one he was given as a child:

Tres Castillos (the three castles) looking northwards along the eastern side of these three rocky hillocks. Victorio and his followers were trapped on the southernmost hill (off camera to the rear of this photograph) Gouyen and Kaywaykla worked their way carefully out of the encircling Mexican state troops using the creep and freeze technique during the night. It is probable that they worked their way through the many scattered boulders from left to right along the base of this side of the Tres Castillos until they reached the gap between the central and right hills. They passed over the saddle between these two hills (the notch in the middle left of the photograph) and eventually rendezvoused with the survivors in the nearest mountains to the west. (Author's photo)

Not until a boy insulted me did I go to Grandmother for an explanation.

"It is true that your name is Spanish, but you have no drop of white blood. Your grandfather lived long among the Mexicans, but you need not be ashamed, for you are pure Apache blood. When you are older you will have an Indian name, but not until you have deserved it."

"How can I earn another name?"

"First by obedience. An Apache obeys or dies. Not only his life but that of the tribe may depend upon his obedience and his truthfulness. In all your life nobody has ever struck you. Nobody will, unless you fail in the things that mean safety to the group. Few Apaches ever strike a child, but for disobedience and lying they must, in order to protect the lives of all."

Vaguely I comprehended these things.

"Above all, you must be truthful. If you are you will be respected; and without respect no human relationship is of any value. No liar is permitted to give evidence in a trial, although he may have witnessed what occurred. No liar is ever permitted to carry messages for fear that he may endanger the whole tribe by not giving his message truthfully. The liar is despised by all.

"And you must be useful and observant. You see how the older boys compete for the honor of serving the warriors. They care for the horses, run the errands, cook the food, and try to anticipate and supply the needs of him whom they serve. They listen respectfully and ask no questions unless they are necessary for obeying commands. They eat poor food, fast for long intervals, are faithful in every way, and above all, do not discuss things they may overhear."

"When may I begin this training?"

"You have already begun it. I've taught you these things since I took you and released your mother to go on the warpath with your father. Continue to practice these things faithfully if you wish to become a warrior. Just this morning you showed plainly that you did not want to break the ice in the little stream and bathe with the older boys."

I was ashamed. I had shrunk from that ordeal, although I had finally endured it. (Ball, 1970, pp.28–29.)

The above passage is very revealing in a number of ways. The virtues of obedience, trust, initiative and observation were all emphasized to children from a very early age. The penalties for failure – including social exclusion – were also clearly outlined and quietly, but firmly, reinforced by comment from the surrounding adults. What is also very clear is that women also took a leading role in reinforcing this basic training. The mentioned breaking ice in mountain streams was one of the ways in which Chiricahua boys would be toughened up for the hard life of a warrior. Daklugie, son of Juh, recalled having to do this in the Sierra Madre supervised by a stern Geronimo who was unprepared to brook any shirking. He also remembered that Geronimo never had to resort to using the stick he carried to enforce his orders.[5]

Other endurance training involved running for long distances with a mouthful of water, the purpose of which was to practise breathing through the nose rather than the mouth. Many other skills of survival and concealment would be picked up during the routine of camp life. The young Apaches would be shown how to locate water and to select the least obvious cover for concealment, as the thickest cover would be the first place an enemy would search. They would hear the arrangements made to scatter and rendezvous at a specific point should the camp be attacked. The children were taught to keep a small supply of food in a pouch around their neck and to keep their blanket so that they would to be able to survive on their own for short periods if, during such an attack, they became temporarily separated from the adults as the Apaches scattered. The Apaches routinely cached surplus supplies such as dried food, textiles, utensils, guns and ammunition throughout their territory in order to be able to quickly replace any losses should their camp be surprised and supplies lost. Again, the children would have seen this happening and had the reasons for these practices explained to them. Kaywaykla also recalled being allowed, along with other boys, to very occasionally fire a rifle with the help of his step-father Kaytennae: "If we got far enough from camp that there was little danger of discovery,[6] he permitted us to practice with his rifle. He knelt behind me to hold the weapon, but let me sight and pull the trigger. Scarcity of ammunition prevented much practice with firearms." (Ball, 1970, p159.)

This picture shows how the terrain almost swallows the Apache youth hunting for squirrels with his bow and arrow. It shows how Apaches could conceal themselves at close range to an enemy. The hunting of squirrels would develop stealth, as these creatures are very shy. Their speed and agility would make them good target practice for an aspiring Apache warrior. As squirrels are also preyed upon by rattlesnakes, hunting squirrels would also provide good practice at spotting and avoiding snakes. (Photo courtesy of National Archaeological Archives, Smithsonian)

5   See Debo, 1976, p.195.
6   This particular practice occurred while on the San Carlos reservation, so the intention was to minimize the possibility of discovery by reservation employees supervising the Chiricahua Apaches. Nevertheless, such practice, on or off reservation, was fraught with the danger of discovery and it would be routine for target practice, on the rare occasions that there was sufficient ammunition, to be carried out away from camp.

In other words, the Apache equivalent of basic training was embedded in the everyday upbringing of the children.

Finally, through Kaywaykla's grandmother, we get an insight into how a growing Apache boy would try to gain the attention of the warriors. If he could develop a reputation for reliability among his seniors an adolescent boy would volunteer for, and be accepted as, an apprentice warrior and so accompany the warriors on a raid. If the youth was seen to have passed his apprenticeship he would be regarded as a fully fledged warrior. To achieve this status the apprentice had to take part in four raids. From a European point of view successful transition to warrior status could be seen as the "coming of age" of a Chiricahua Apache youth. The word used by the Chiricahua Apaches was *dikohe*, which Opler and Hoijer translate as "novice on the raid or war-path." (Opler & Hoijer, 1940, p.618.) In practice, the experience of the *dikohe* was wider than accompanying warriors on four raids:

> My father did his best to bring me out just as he was brought out when he was a young boy. He trained me as he was trained, gave me all the ceremonial training he had been through once himself. When I was ten or twelve years old he began to teach me and was very strict with me. He would say to me, "You must have your arrows and bow where you can grab them. You must have your knife right beside you. You must have your moccasins right beside you. Be on the alert in peace or in war. Don't spend all your time sleeping. Get up when the morning star comes out. Watch for the morning star. Don't let it get up before you do." (Opler & Hoijer, 1940, p.618.)

Opler and Hoijer confirm that the general toughening up of aspiring Apache warriors commenced around puberty and ended when they had completed their fourth raid. However, Kaywaykla's account above shows that before this period younger boys would be actively encouraged to take part in this toughening process. The other point made by Opler and Hoijer was that the *dikohe* training was not standardized within the Chiricahua Apaches and that many variations could occur between individual families. This training would, however, usually be mediated by an outsider respected by the family.[7]

The critical aspect of becoming a *dikohe* was that this was a period during which disobedience of one's elders would not be tolerated. All manner of physical tests were routinely sprung on the *dikohe* and he would be expected to complete them without question. The *dikohe* would not dare to refuse, as this would be noted, and his chances of being ultimately selected to go on a raid would be dashed, as the acceptance of an aspiring apprentice warrior was by no means guaranteed. If the warriors judged the applicant to be less than reliable in the key traits of obedience, trustworthiness, etc. then he would not be accepted as an apprentice. It is not quite clear what happened if a youth failed to be accepted; the likelihood is that while he would probably be tolerated there would be little chance of social advance. There are a number of accounts of what are termed "bronco Apaches" and pre-1886 these appear to refer to adult males who had seriously transgressed the rules.

---

[7] In fact, Opler and Hoijer provide an excellent guide to the training of a Chiricahua Apache apprentice warrior and while I shall try to do their work justice over the space of a couple of pages there is no substitute for reading the original article. See the further reading section at the end of this book.

However, one could see how failure to measure up during the *dikohe* training might produce the occasional bronco Apache.

If accepted, there was quite a clear set of rituals designed to test the applicant's resolve and suitability for warrior status. In the first place, his family would try to discourage him by outlining the dangers with which he would be confronted on a raid. If this did not shake the youth's resolve, then a shaman would outline the apprentice's spiritual responsibilities and instruct him on the use of certain equipment unique to the apprentice warrior. The shaman would also clearly warn the apprentice of the dire consequences, both to the apprentice and to the other members of the raiding party, of being found wanting on the four raiding trips. Any failings would potentially mark the aspiring warrior as being unreliable, untrustworthy or even dangerous to his fellow Apaches. The young Apache was continually exposed to tales and myths designed to reinforce the virtues of obedience, trust, forbearance, respect for one's elders, initiative and observation. Such morality tales were a key ingredient of a culture that intended to produce tough and disciplined guerrilla warfare experts.

In keeping with this, the apprentice had to follow a series of ritual practices and beliefs while accompanying the warriors on the four raids. First and foremost, it was made clear to the *dikohe* that he was not expected to take part in the raid. He was there to serve the warriors and to act as an observer. Thus, the menial work of the camp was his domain and he had to be prepared to be at the beck and call of any of the warriors. Even if good food was available, he was expected to abstain from eating the best cuts of

TRAINING – FINAL MOONRISE PREPARATIONS FOR A RAID

In this training scene an Apache *dikohe* (**1**), can be seen wearing breechclout, belt with knife, cotton shirt and trousers, headband and boots. He is carrying a bow and his quiver is slung in the "march" position. He is holding the reins of five horses belonging to the raiding party (**2**). The leader of the raiding party (**3**) is dressed in breechclout, boots and headband with his quiver and bow swung in the "active" position. He holds a Sharps carbine in the crook of his arm and carries a cartridge belt. He is giving the apprentice warrior final instructions as to where to make for if the raid went according to plan. Another warrior (**4**) keeps an eye upon the distant intended target, a Mexican hacienda complex (**8**), which was most probably chosen because of the fiesta under way – if the Apaches knew of such an event they might choose to steal some horses, hoping that the guard would be somewhat lax. The warrior is peering between two rocks so as not to silhouette himself against the skyline. He is also watching a signal fire (**7**) on the mountain range many miles away. The signal fire would have been lit, in a prearranged location, by a scout sent on ahead with instructions to survey the target. One lit fire would indicate that the raiding party should execute their raid, whereas two lit fires would be used to warn them off.

One of the warriors (**5**), armed with a lance, flop-headed war club and slung bow and quiver, sets out towards the target. The final warrior of the party (**6**) has swung round and is waiting for (**5**) to join him. He is armed with an Enfield musket and slung bow and quiver. He is below any line of sight from the hacienda as there is a thick wood of pines and mountain oaks just below his position. The raiding party are going to use this cover to approach as closely to the hacienda as possible. He is dressed in a poncho and Mexican sombrero. Apaches were known to try to pass themselves off as Mexicans in order to evade or, in this case, get as close to any sentry as possible without raising suspicion.

An obvious landmark, in this case a standing rock (**9**), would have been chosen as a rendezvous point if the raid was successful. If the raid should go wrong, the warriors would rendezvous at another, far more distant, site. It should be noted that while it would be unusual for Apaches to fight at night, it was not so unusual for them to use night to close in on a target for a raid. The aim of this raid would not have been to fight a full skirmish but to spirit away horses, with the odd sentry being knocked out or killed in the process.

food and to eat the food cold and in moderation. This was accompanied by the statement that to disobey these strictures would destroy any power he had over horses. These practices were a means by which the apprentice would become acclimatized to the worst privations a raiding party might have to deal with if things went wrong. This was backed up with tales of dire moral consequences should the *dikohe* fail to adhere to these practices.

Other examples of ritual practices included the use of the drinking tube and the scratching stick and often the wearing of a buckskin hat by the apprentice warrior. The scratching stick and drinking tube were carried on the belt and again their use was accompanied by the direst warnings concerning the failure to use them. If the *dikohe* allowed water to touch his lips then he would grow facial hair, which the Chiricahuas considered extremely ugly. If he scratched his head without using his stick then his skin would lose its toughness. Once more, the purpose behind these rules was to test the basic discipline and concentration of the apprentice warrior.

The buckskin cap worn by the apprentice warrior was made by a man known to have "power" to ensure the safety of the *dikohe* through the making of such hats. One of Opler and Hoijer's informants told them that:

> The hat was yellow with a black zig-zag design on it representative of the lightning. For his second expedition a blue design was substituted. The third time a white figure was put on, and on the fourth trip the hat was decorated with a yellow lightning symbol. The black, blue, white and yellow of the design stood for the east, south, west and north respectively ... which constitutes the Apache ceremonial circuit. (Opler & Hoijer, 1940, p.622.)

While the apprentice was being tested, some elements of the rituals and beliefs surrounding his raiding experience were intended to promote his safety. The dangers facing the apprentice were very real, the clearest being when a raid went wrong and the raiders had to fight. Every attempt would be made to keep the *dikohe* out of harm's way, but apprentice warriors were sometimes killed during their novitiate. The loss of an aspiring warrior would usually, depending upon the specific circumstances, reflect badly upon the accompanying warriors, particularly the leader of the raid. Thus, while an apprentice might be treated as a camp servant during a raid, the warriors had a clear responsibility to take every step to ensure the survival of their *dikohe*. If it were judged that an apprentice warrior had been lost unnecessarily, then the leader of the raiding party stood to lose his position of respect and lose most or all of his following. Therefore, deciding to take an apprentice was a risky venture for a raiding party and explains why the adults, such as Kaywaykla's grandmother, would keep a close day-to-day eye upon the attitude and behavior of children and adolescents. Any doubts as to the reliability of a potential warrior would almost certainly destroy any chance of them being selected as a *dikohe*. If, once selected, an apprentice did not measure up, then he would not be taken on any further raids and his social standing would be destroyed.

The most important skill that an apprentice had to learn was a special vocabulary that would be used by the *dikohe* during the raid. For example, one of Opler and Hoijer's informants stated that "Instead of saying 'I want to drink some water,' we had to say, 'I begin to swim the specular iron ore.'" (Opler & Hoijer, 1940, p.623) and "A mule, for instance, is called a 'tail dragger.'" (Opler in Eggan, 1955, p.232.)

Opler and Hoijer noted that it was not clear if both the *dikohe* and the warriors used this language, and concluded on the balance of probability that it was only the apprentice who utilized it. This would make sense, as it appears that the purpose of the exercise was to see how much complex information a *dikohe* could assimilate and remember in a relatively short space of time. If he were successful in remembering and correctly using this language over the space of four raids, then he could be trusted to remember complex instruction and planning as a fully-fledged warrior embarking upon a raid or going out to make war upon his enemies.

If the *dikohe* completed the four raids to the satisfaction of the warriors, he was accepted as an adult warrior. As such, he would be free to marry and smoke, but from the point of view of his new warrior peer group he was no longer to be protected but was expected to engage fully in any raid or war in which he volunteered his participation.

A final comment made by one of Opler and Hoijer's informants is revealing and demonstrates that before the *dikohe* actually ventured on their first raid they were already very well prepared: "In fact, many a young boy at fourteen was as well trained and dangerous as a soldier." (Opler & Hoijer, 1940, p.618.) In other words, the key period for producing the Chiricahua Apache warrior was from mid to late childhood into adolescence. It involved an intensive training program accompanied by the teaching of a series of cultural beliefs and practices that underlined the rationale behind that training regime.

LEADERSHIP

The first point that can be made about leadership within the Chiricahua Apaches stems from the strict training of the *dikohe*. At first glance, the strict obedience enforced upon the apprentice warriors by this training program would appear to act against the development of the sophisticated and flexible guerrilla warfare techniques alluded to earlier.

However, one has to realize that each adult Chiricahua warrior was a leader in his own right. The minimum family group could consist of one fully trained warrior, his immediate female kin and male and female offspring. As such, even if this individual did not aspire to lead other Chiricahua warriors on a raid or in battle he was still responsible for his own survival and that of his immediate family group. Thus, on a daily basis the individual warrior had to be an alert, adaptable individual.

Nevertheless, the immediate family groups provided the building blocks for individuals such as Cochise, Mangas Coloradas, Victorio, Juh, Nana, Chihuahua, Jolsanny (also known as Ulzana) and Kaytennae to rise to the position of leading relatively large numbers of Chiricahua Apache warriors.

The basic condition of leadership was success in raiding and warfare. Those leaders able to maintain this success could still be seen leading their warriors to a great age. Nana was believed to be approximately 75 years old when he led his raid into New Mexico in 1881. Jolsanny was believed to be in his late sixties when he directed his raid in November and December 1885. The only reason that these leaders were still in power was because they had been able to maintain their reputation for success. This success was usually judged on the basis of whether the minimum loss (ideally no losses) had been

Chato, a famous, though controversial, Chiricahua warrior who was at first hostile but then signed up as a scout for the US Army. The interesting feature of this photograph is that, at first glance, he is holding a Springfield carbine. However, the barrel is much longer than carbine barrels in earlier photographs. This rifle may be a Springfield rifle with the wood cut back or a carbine with a replacement barrel. (Photo courtesy of National Archaeological Archives, Smithsonian)

sustained for the maximum damage inflicted upon the enemy. However, this was not quite as straightforward as it might first appear. A raid designed to capture 20 horses from a particular hacienda might be judged a failure if a single warrior was perceived to have been lost unnecessarily. If one remembers that the basic social unit of the Chiricahua Apache was the immediate family unit, the unnecessary loss of a warrior could have an immediate impact upon that group's economic well-being. Thus, on November 13, 1882, when the Chiricahua Apaches trapped and killed Mexican commander Juan Mata Ortiz and 21 other Mexican soldiers, they did not hold a victory celebration as the loss of two warriors to gain such a victory was seen as too costly.

A younger warrior could quickly garner the support of the warriors from closely related family groups by building up a reputation for success in raiding and warfare. If he maintained this success he could even rise to prominence in one of the sub-divisions of the Chiricahua (Chokonen, Chihenne, Nehdni or Bedonkohe) or beyond. This perceived success had to be maintained and could suddenly be lost, though there was no hard and fast rule as to what would lose a leader support. Juh, often seen as the leading man of the Nehdni from the 1860s through to 1883, seems to have lost his position as a result of a surprise attack upon his camp by Mexican troops during which his wife was killed. In following the attackers he lost four warriors who were killed in the subsequent skirmish. Victorio suffered a heavy defeat at the hands of Apache scouts in May 1880 but did not lose his position of authority. In both incidents it was the perception of the leader's followers that led to him either losing or retaining support. Juh was clearly judged to have been at fault whereas Victorio seems to have been exonerated of any blame by the majority of his followers.

Leadership was not hereditary, though Sweeney argues that the offspring of a successful leader might find themselves better placed for future leadership simply by dint of the training received from their father. If a new leader was required he would usually be elected from among the warriors. Being the son of a previous leader might give a candidate an advantage but this would soon be lost if the successful candidate failed to develop a reputation for minimizing losses and maximizing gains. Being elected leader did not necessarily grant wide-ranging power. Opler stated that successful leadership was "a process in which birth and wealth have their place, but in which ability and personal magnetism are always the leavening factor." (Opler, 1996, p.470.) The role of leader in Apache society would be achieved through a warrior's record as a raider and warrior. However, this role also involved being an effective mediator between the various family groups who accepted his leadership; a leader would be expected to speak publicly on important matters but the rest of his following was under no duty to follow his advice. Nevertheless, a leader's word was likely to carry more weight with his audience than that of any other individual. Thus, if individuals in his following came into conflict it would often be the leader who would try to step in to avoid bloodshed, or at the very least to minimize the bloodshed. If such conflict happened in a large group of Apaches the overall leader could often count on the backing of the leaders of smaller family units who had chosen to follow him.

However, Apache leaders whose positions were seriously challenged were by no means helpless; if they had retained a high level of support within their following, leadership challenges could quickly become lethal. Victorio shot dead a leading allied Mescalero Apache leader called Ca-bal-le-so, preventing those Mescalero Apaches allied to his cause leaving him. The result of this incident was that less than a month later these Mescalero Apaches sustained about half the casualties when Victorio was trapped and killed at Tres Castillos. In 1876, the sons of Cochise, Taza and Naiche were faced by a leadership challenge from Eskinya and Pionsenay. They gunned down and killed Eskinya and seriously wounded Pionsenay in a murderous exchange at point-blank range.

A key element of Chiricahua Apache leadership was also the perception that the leader was endowed with some form of power. The clearest picture left by Apache informants concerns two Chihenne: Nana and Lozen, Victorio's sister. However, there is some information given about others such as Juh, Chihuahua and Geronimo himself. Before these examples are examined in detail it should be noted that this concept is, for a contemporary audience whose education is heavily influenced by notions of scientific rationalism, quite difficult to pin down. Ball, Sanchez and Henn point out that: "Power is a mysterious, intangible attribute difficult to explain, even by one possessing it. It was, even above his courage, the most valuable attribute of a chief." Their informants also pointed out that the Chiricahua Apaches believed that an individual could use their power for good or ill. Witchcraft, to the Chiricahua Apaches, was the conscious misuse of power to do another person harm.

Both Juh and Geronimo were believed to have the power to tell the future. Jason Betzinez, one of Geronimo's apprentice warriors in 1882–83, recorded a number of such instances. On one occasion Geronimo correctly predicted the arrival of some Mexican troops who duly appeared the following day, as and when predicted. The most interesting incident recorded by Betzinez was when Geronimo, in camp far away from their base camp in the Sierra Madre, suddenly sat up and announced that US troops had taken their camp. As it turned out, General Crook's 1883 expedition into the Sierra Madre Mountains had surprised the Chiricahua Apaches who had taken refuge in these rugged Mexican mountains. In later life, Betzinez made every effort to assimilate into US society and consciously rejected the beliefs of his upbringing, a stance which did not endear him to some other Chiricahua Apaches. However, he noted that, many years after this event, he simply could not explain how Geronimo knew their camp had been taken.

Chihuahua was believed to have power over horses to the extent that he could calm the wildest of horses. Nana was said to have power over rattlesnakes and ammunition. In the latter case, this power translated into the belief that if Nana was present on a raid designed to garner fresh ammunition then a supply of fresh cartridges would be found.

Finally Lozen, Victorio's sister, was believed to have the power to locate enemies who were too close for comfort. She would slowly revolve with arms spread wide with her palms upward. If there were enemies close by: "As she turned slowly, following the sun, her hands tingled and the palms changed color when they pointed toward the foe. The intensity of the sensation indicated the approximate distance of the enemy. The closer the adversary, the more vivid the feeling." (Ball, 1970, p.11.)

James Kaywaykla remembered seeing Lozen doing this many times and firmly believed that had she been with Victorio he would never have been caught at Tres Castillos. No matter what a non-Chiricahua Apache audience might make of these beliefs, the concept of a leader's "power" was clearly a key element of their leadership's success. The fact that Nana, Chihuahua, Lozen and Geronimo maintained their reputations until the end of the Apache Wars means that nothing happened to shake their followers' beliefs in the efficacy of their power. If that had happened, these individuals would have lost their leadership role and have escaped the attention of history. As noted earlier, Juh appears to have been perceived to have lost his power. However, one of Ball's main informants was Juh's last surviving son, Daklugie, so Juh's reputation has been preserved for history.

A final comment upon the influence of an important leader is that if he was killed then revenging his death was not just a matter for his immediate family, but his entire following, and all were expected to exact vengeance.

These two photographs of the same Apache warrior show the increasing influence of European/Mexican dress upon the Apaches. Despite this influence, the long hair, breechclout, headband and boots are retained even after the addition of a fine waistcoat. The photos also show a flop-headed war club and a bow, giving a good idea of the relative proportions of these weapons. The warrior would also have added a couple of cartridge belts, at least one knife and possibly a revolver. (Photos courtesy of National Archaeological Archives, Smithsonian)

APPEARANCE

We are, at first glance, fortunate to have some excellent photographic studies of Apache warriors taken in the 1870s and 1880s. The most famous of these would be the series of images recorded by C. S. Fly during General George Crook's negotiations with Chiricahua Apaches led by Geronimo and Naiche at Cañon de los Embudos in March 1886. However, it is clear from Apache testimony that, if warriors knew that they were going to go into battle, they would usually strip down to the minimum of clothing and equipment. As a witness to the battle between the Chiricahua Apaches and the 4th Cavalry in Horseshoe Canyon in April 1882, Betzinez noted that prior to fighting the warriors all removed their shirts. Thus a Chiricahua Apache warrior would tend to fight wearing boots, breechclout and headband plus whatever equipment, such as belts or quivers, he happened to need for fighting. The removal of surplus clothing would suggest that the Apaches were aware of

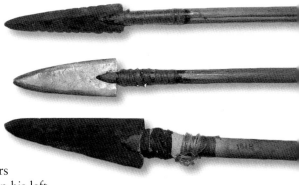

the dangers of infection caused by cloth fragments lodged in bullet wounds. Therefore, in many of the photographs taken of Chiricahua Apaches they are probably wearing the Apache equivalent of their "Sunday best" and the resulting photographs do not necessarily reflect exactly what they would look like in battle.

This is not to say that these photographs have no value. For example the famous shot of Geronimo and Naiche, mounted on horses and flanked by two warriors on foot, one of whom is holding an infant balanced upon his left hip, shows some very interesting detail. The warrior on foot to the right is wearing a jacket and what appears to be a "fireman's shirt." In battle he would probably have taken off both but would have retained the two cartridge belts, breechclout, boots, necklace and headband. The ammunition clearly visible in one of the belts suggests that he would be armed with a Springfield 45/70 rifle or 45/55 carbine. The empty ammunition belt looks designed to hold revolver ammunition and suggests that he was also armed with a revolver. The other dismounted warrior would have retained the same clothing and equipment as the first, having gotten rid of the waistcoat and, if time allowed, the cotton leggings. He too has two cartridge belts and both appear to be filled with Springfield carbine/rifle ammunition. The edge of what might be a flap holster appears to be hanging from his left side. A good knife would be carried at all times, though none are visible in this particular photo.

The boots worn by the Apaches were more than just protection against the many thorns and spines encountered in the flora of Apacheria; they could also hold small objects such as awls and thread (natural or woven) for repairing the boots. The drinking straw and scratching stick mentioned earlier as part of the equipment of an apprentice warrior were said to have been strung together and attached to the *dikohe*'s belt.

The basic dress of high boots, breechclout and headband and the carrying of a knife remained unchanged from 1860 to 1886, though there was also an increase in the wearing of European hats as an alternative to the headband over the period.

Examples of different Apache arrowheads. The different means by which individual fletchers would attach the arrowheads to the shafts of the arrows can be seen. (Author's photo – courtesy of access given by the AHS)

EQUIPMENT

The period 1860–86 shows an interesting pattern of both continuity and change amongst the equipment carried by the Chiricahua Apache warrior. In the early 1860s the bow and arrow, lance, flop-headed war club, musket, occasional Sharps carbine and the very occasional Spencer or Henry repeating rifle could be seen. This sort of equipment meant that the Chiricahua Apaches relied upon more immediate hit and run tactics unless they had their enemies at the most extreme disadvantage.

The Chiricahua Apache bow was between three and four feet long and the preferred source was wood from the mulberry tree. Smaller bows for hunting birds and rodents were also made, but usually given to boys to help them develop their shooting skills in preparation for using the full-sized bow. There were two types of arrow: "those of carrizo or reed into which a hardwood foreshaft is fitted and those with the entire shaft of hardwood."

An arrowhead made from a barrel hoop. Part of the hole by which the hoop would have been pinned to the barrel can still be seen. (Photo by Eric Fuller – courtesy of access given by the Romero Collection)

ABOVE LEFT
Two Apache arrowheads found in the vicinity of Massacre Gap (also known as Massacre Peak), New Mexico, where Apache warriors wiped out a Mexican carreta train in October 1879. If the tip of the arrowhead to the right is carefully examined, one can see that it is slightly bent backwards. Thus, if the arrow hit or glanced off bone the tip would tend to bend or even break off making it even harder to withdraw from the wound. (Karl Laumbach)

ABOVE RIGHT
The same two arrowheads compared with an Apache arrowhead found in Hembrillo Canyon, San Andres Mountains, New Mexico, where the US army fought the Apaches in April 1880. The Hembrillo arrowhead shows an even more prominent bent back point which would have been very difficult to withdraw without causing further damage. (Karl Laumbach – inclusion of Hembrillo arrowhead courtesy of White Sands Missile Range)

BELOW
The manufacture of arrowheads was accomplished by chiselling the point into a rough point and then it was filed down to its final shape. This process did not always reach fruition and the one below is an example of an unfinished point where the warrior decided that his initial shaping of the arrowhead had failed and discarded to be found by archaeologists over a century later. (Photo by John Fitch courtesy of Karl Laumbach and the Cañada Alamosa Project)

(Opler, 1996, p.388.) The carrizo or reed arrows were slightly longer (approximately 30 inches long) than arrows made wholly from hardwood. Opler also noted that warriors would usually carry between 30 and 40 arrows and keep a fresh supply in camp. The size and shape of arrowheads seem to vary, but all were attached to the shaft by splitting the shaft and holding the arrowhead in place with tightly wrapped sinew.

Opler also noted that the bow and arrows would be decorated as follows:

> The outer surface [of the bow] is usually painted a solid color; on the inner surface the maker puts a design by which his handiwork is known – a star, a cross, serrated lines, parallel lines or a naturalistic figure. This may refer to his supernatural power or may be simply a decoration or an identification mark… the shaft [of the arrow]… is decorated with bands of black, blue or red paint. On the upper portion of the shaft, at about the middle of the area which will be covered by the feathers, a narrow band of green or red is often traced. (Opler, 1996, pp.387–388.)

By the 1860s the Chiricahuas rarely used stone arrow heads.

Chiricahua Apache lances would be made either from the Sotol plant or spruce. The shaft would be cleaned and left out to dry. By the 1860s the blades of knives or broken-off sabre blades would be used for the head of the lance. The length of the shaft would be between five and seven feet. According to Opler, the lance was not thrown but used as a two-handed weapon on foot.

At the beginning of the 1860s, the Chiricahua Apaches would also carry what is known as a flop-headed war club. A round stone would be wrapped in flexible rawhide and attached to a shaft of wood. The wooden handle would often be decorated with buckskin and horsehair, or a cow's tail could be attached to the base of the shaft. In hand-to-hand combat a skilled warrior could make full use of the slingshot effect of the flexible attachment of the head of the club by stopping a downward blow just short of the target's head.

As breech-loading and repeating arms, accompanied by metallic cartridges, came into more common usage, the Chiricahua Apaches developed far more aggressive tactics. They would be more likely to hold a good defensive position against well-armed opponents; maintain their positions during a successful ambush; and even launch flowing counterattacks, infiltrating towards and around their foes using the terrain and the ease with which their weapons could be reloaded to "psyche-out" their opponents. However, for these tactics to work they needed to have a good supply of ammunition. By the 1870s and 1880s the Chiricahua Apaches, by rapidly

adopting the modern weaponry developed by the USA, transformed themselves into far more dangerous opponents than ever before.

The Chiricahua Apache warriors of 1860 were fearsome adversaries, if allowed to dictate the conditions of the conflict. However, with the advent of new weapons technology they were able to widen the range of options through which they could attempt to determine such conditions. By 1882, Betzinez recorded that: "The older warriors were using single-shot Springfields of the Civil War pattern while the younger ones were armed with repeating rifles – Winchesters and Marlins. In addition many of the men had pistols and other miscellaneous firearms which had been taken in raids on the settlements or attacks on travelers [sic] on the lonely roads in Arizona and New Mexico." (Betzinez, 1959, p.77.)

This pattern in the distribution of modern rifles types also reveals something suggested by the archeological record of battles between the US Army and Apaches in 1880. It would appear that the Apaches, through their appreciation of the relative pros and cons of single-shot carbines/rifles and repeating rifles/carbines, deployed these weapons in order to maximize their advantages and minimize their drawbacks. At Hembrillo Canyon it was discovered that the Apaches had tended to deploy their single-shot Springfields and a few Remingtons to take advantage of their longer effective ranges. Warriors using these weapons were stationed on ridges further away from their enemies, whilst warriors armed with repeating rifles were used to picket the water source nearest their foes, thus allowing a high rate of fire to be brought down on anyone trying to reach the water. The warriors who launched probing infiltration attacks also tended to be armed with repeating rifles. If the Apaches had enough ammunition, then with the use of rapid fire and movement through difficult terrain the rifles were used to give the impression that there were more warriors present than actually were. It should also be noted that

ABOVE LEFT
The above metal fragments are examples of arrowhead manufacture recently discovered by archaeologists in New Mexico. These are the offcuts from the production of arrowheads left in camp. (Photo by John Fitch courtesy of Karl Laumbach and the Cañada Alamosa Project)

ABOVE RIGHT
The range in size and shape of arrowheads can be seen in this photograph. (Author's photo – courtesy of access given by the Parrish Collection)

BOTTOM LEFT
Lance belonging to the Western Apache leader Alchise. Here, virtually the entire blade of a sword has been used. The lance is held in the archives of the Arizona Historical Society (AHS), Tucson, Arizona. (Author's photo – courtesy of access given by the AHS)

BOTTOM RIGHT
A sotol plant in Magdalena Gap on the Butterfield Trail. The stalk of this plant would be used to make lances. (Author's photo)

Replica of a flop-headed war club. (Author's photo – courtesy of access given by Dan Aranda)

such deployments of types of rifle are a further illustration of the operational thinking that governed the actions of the Chiricahua.

It should also be noted that Betzinez's information also suggests that the deployment of such weapons was also age-related, with the older and relatively less active warriors taking the longer-range weapons while the younger, more active warriors were armed with repeating rifles. Obviously, Chiricahua warriors did not always have the luxury of making these deployments for, as we shall see, one of their main problems was finding a reliable source of rifles and ammunition. Therefore, depending upon availability, young Apaches would happily use single-shot weapons while older Chiricahuas would carry repeating rifles. One should remember that compared with a muzzle-loading musket, single-shot weapons would still allow a far higher rate of fire while on the move if a 16-shot repeating rifle was not available.

Conversely, while lances and bows and arrows would be common weapons in the early 1860s, Betzinez reported that they were rarely used by 1882. However, archeology confirms the use of the bow by the Chiricahua and Mescalero Apaches who attacked Lt. John Conline's Company A, 9th Cavalry, on April 5, 1880. In this case, some Apaches had managed to infiltrate round his right flank and used bows and arrows to target the horses and their guards in an attempt to stampede the company's horses.[8]

As they became available, the Apaches also developed a liking for field glasses. Kaywaykla remembers Victorio using field glasses and Nana was also recorded as carrying a beautiful modern telescope on his famous raid in 1881. The Arizona Historical Society has two fine specimens of field glasses, one carried by General Crook and the other by Geronimo.

---

[8]   The author has seen on this site a marker where an arrowhead was found approximately three feet away from one of the horse guard's spent cartridges.

The Apaches would also use captured materials to replace natural materials. A Texas Ranger report of a skirmish with Mescalero Apaches in Mexico discovered a bag, made out of a shirt sleeve tied off at one end, on the body of a slain Apache. It was filled with approximately 250 rounds of ammunition for a Winchester repeating rifle. There are examples of a small metal file being cut down and fashioned into an awl and small scissors being broken apart to create awls – the awl was an essential item for moccasin repair. Furthermore, there are examples of cartridge cases being fashioned into tweezers and one fascinating example of a cartridge case being fashioned into a powder measure to refill spent cartridges. The Chiricahuas would also use metal barrel hoops to make arrowheads.

ON CAMPAIGN 1860–86

The distinction between raiding and warfare is crucial to understanding the changing nature of warfare for the Chiricahua Apaches between 1860 and 1886. The key factor at play was the increasing development of the Southwest of the USA by Anglo-American ranchers, miners and settlers. By 1870 the ongoing warfare with the Chiricahua Apaches resulted in the US Army beginning to pay more attention to the "Apache problem." It also prompted the Department of the Interior to make overtures of peace to the various groups of hostile Western and Chiricahua Apaches, with the aim of settling the Apaches upon reservations. The key issue for the Chiricahua Apaches, straddling the Mexico-US border, was that pre-1860, if in conflict with the Chihuahuan and/or Sonoran authorities, the Apaches could move northwards and be relatively safe from retaliation from Mexico. With the increasing US political and military commitment to the settlement and development of New Mexico and Arizona, the experience of raiding and warfare changed for the Chiricahua Apaches.

Before the 1860s, raiding and warfare with the Mexicans tended to follow a pattern of regular bouts of raiding and warfare punctuated with periods of truce and trade. This pattern certainly continued with Hispanic communities on the Mexican side of the border up until the surrender of Geronimo in 1886. The Chihennes maintained peaceful trade relations with a number of Hispanic communities in the USA until 1880–81. These relationships came under increasing pressure as the USA increased its involvement in

Small file cut down, sharpened at both ends and used as an awl. (Author's photo – courtesy of access given by the Romero Collection)

the Southwest. After the end of the Civil War the steady increase of the US Army presence in the Southwest meant that the Chiricahua Apaches faced growing pressure upon what had previously been their relatively safe heartland. Thus, raiding and warfare against the USA became a much more drawn out affair, and leaders such as Cochise in the 1860s and Victorio as late as 1880[9] were forced to sustain campaigns over months and years. This was because the Americans were pushing into every part of the territory and it became increasingly difficult for the Chiricahua Apaches to maintain such safe havens. It was the steady attrition of a warrior lost here and a warrior crippled there that persuaded the Chiricahua Apaches to meet with peace envoys from the USA in 1871 and to accept two reservations – one centred around Fort Bowie in Arizona and one based at Old Fort Tularosa, which was then moved to Ojo Caliente in New Mexico. The transition was not always smooth, with many warriors continuing to raid the surrounding area. However, it was the policy of concentrating the Western and Chiricahua Apaches upon one reservation in Arizona that led to the last ten years of the Apache Wars.

The Fort Bowie reservation was closed in 1876 and a number of Chiricahua Apaches (some of the Chokonens and most of the Nehdnis) did not accept the move to San Carlos and tried to reclaim their independence by resuming their independent way of life in both the USA and Mexico. The Ojo Caliente reservation proved to be a useful rendezvous point where plunder, mainly

[9] As late as 1879, a local New Mexican newspaper warned its readers that to prospect for minerals in the Black Range and San Mateo Mountains of New Mexico was at the prospector's own risk. It should be noted that this was after the Chihenne Apaches had been twice removed to San Carlos reservation in 1877 and 1878.

EQUIPMENT

As well as his weapons, the Apache warrior could carry a variety of equipment. The powder scoop (**1**) was fashioned from a spent cartridge. It would be used to measure out powder used to refill used cartridges. Bullet or ball moulds could be used to cast a new bullet or ball and then the scoop would be used to fill the cartridge case before the bullet was inserted. The reliability of such refilled cartridges varied. Despite this, given a choice between no ammunition or refill ammunition, the Apaches chose the latter.

Probably one of the most important pieces of equipment for an Apache warrior was the awl. It was originally made using sharpened bone fragments or thorns. However, contact with Europeans introduced a whole range of metal implements that could be fashioned into awls. The ability to carry out running repairs or make new boots on campaign was essential if the Apache warrior was to protect his feet and be able to keep moving over the stony and thorny terrain of the Southwest. The awls shown have been made from a variety of objects: a cut-down small metal file (**2**); a cut-down pair of scissors (**3**); and a horseshoe nail (**4**).

Tweezers (**5 & 6**) were also an important part of the Chiricahua Apache's equipment. Facial hair was seen to be ugly and to reflect some form of character flaw. Thus, any self-respecting warrior or apprentice would want to remove any sign of a moustache or beard. In this case, a spent cartridge has been flattened and split to form a set of tweezers which would be worn around the neck.

While the Apaches knew how use pitch to make waterproof baskets (**7 & 8**) for carrying water, they also used cleaned-out horse entrails to carry water. A European-made canteen, either US Army (**9**) or civilian (**10 & 11**) would have been a prized possession of the Apache warrior. These could be acquired by trade or taken in war.

Field glasses or telescopes became prized possessions of the Apache warrior as they valued anything that could improve their surveillance of their surroundings. These could be obtained through trading or raiding. Here can be seen field glasses that belonged to General George Crook (**12**) and those belonging to Geronimo (**13**).

Geronimo's Springfield rifle (top) and a Spencer repeating rifle (bottom) believed to have been used by an Apache warrior. Both rifles have been modified before falling into Apache hands. The Springfield rifle has been shortened, probably for ease of mounted and dismounted use. The Spencer has a much heavier hexagonal barrel added. The bottom photo shows this feature more clearly. The hexagonal barrel makes the weapon much heavier, but it being longer probably increases the rifle's effective range. This weapon ties in nicely with the earlier photo of Chato with what looks like a Springfield carbine with an exaggerated barrel. This was probably a photographer's prop, as the famous picture of Geronimo kneeling scowling into the camera appears to use the same weapon. There was clearly gunsmith knowledge amongst the Apaches' European opponents and such customizations were sometimes traded or captured by the Chiricahua Apaches. (Photos by Frank Brito (top), Bernd Brand (middle) and the author (bottom) courtesy of access given by the AHS)

taken in Mexico, could be sold. This outlet was closed when the Chihenne were moved to San Carlos in 1877. The resistance to this move by political means (through Loco) and military means (spearheaded by Victorio until his death in October 1880 and Nana until 1881) culminated in one of the most punishing campaigns against the Chiricahua Apaches between 1879 and 1881. The resistance by the Chihenne leaders to the loss of their Ojo Caliente reservation did an enormous amount of damage in the Southwest and in Chihuahua, but by 1881 it was clear to the surviving independent Chihennes that they could no longer maintain their old way of life in territory claimed by the USA. Those Chokonen and Nehdnis who did not accept the move to San Carlos in 1876 had, thanks to increasing military pressure from Sonora and Chihuahua periodically aided by the Federal Mexican Army, negotiated a move to San Carlos by January 1880. The ensuing peace with the Nehdnis and Chokonen lasted until the aftermath of an Apache scout mutiny in August 1881, when the increased military presence on the reservation prompted many Nehdnis and Chokonen, fearing treachery, to flee south to the Sierra Madre Mountains in Mexico. There they united with the Chihennes under Nana. The 1882–83 period marks the efforts of these Chiricahua Apaches to maintain their independence in northern Mexico.

General George Crook's expedition into the Sierra Madre in 1883 persuaded most of the Chiricahua Apaches that this was not a viable option and most had returned to San Carlos by February 1884. The Geronimo Campaign of 1885–86 was a last-gasp effort by some Chiricahua Apaches to maintain their independence in the face of a daunting cocktail of internal division and a well-meaning, but probably too rapid, imposition of an alien way of life upon them.

Although ultimately defeated, the Chiricahua Apache on campaign was a formidable opponent, particularly considering the small number of warriors involved in hostilities. In the most damaging period of

warfare between the USA and the Chiricahua Apaches, 1879–81, Victorio probably led a maximum of 150 Chihennes and allied Chiricahua and Mescalero Apaches. Despite the odds being against the Apaches, it took the USA and Mexico a long time to wear down their resistance. This was due to the techniques employed by the Apaches when on a prolonged campaign. There were a number of factors at play including: the principle of maximum damage for minimal loss; knowledge of the terrain; the role of women; the siting of campsites; long-range communication; illicit trade networks; and an inherent squad leader system. The following pages will look at each factor in turn.

Maximum damage for minimum loss

The Chiricahua Apaches' ethos of maximum gain for minimum loss meant that they avoided direct conflict unless they had carried out what we might call a thorough risk assessment of the advantages and disadvantages of any attack. This could involve careful long-term monitoring of enemy routines to identify the strengths and weaknesses of a possible target. If this reconnaissance did not show any weakness that could be sufficiently exploited then no attack would be made. Military patrols sent after, or in search of, Chiricahua Apaches would generally be avoided and only attacked if circumstances were particularly favorable. An example of this is General George Crook's successful demonstration of the use of Apache scouts in the early 1870s, which had an obvious effect upon a Chiricahua leader such as Nana. When Nana led his six-week raid into New Mexico in 1881, a clear pattern emerged: when he was confronted by US forces accompanied by Apache scouts he made every effort to evade the scouts as quickly as possible. Conversely, the three 9th Cavalry detachments that his warriors did attack were not accompanied by Apache scouts. All three detachments sustained serious casualties, both horses and men, and took no further part in the pursuit of Nana.

Knowledge of the terrain

As part of this risk-aware approach the Chiricahuas used their knowledge of the terrain to both ensure their survival and to engineer the downfall of their enemies. They knew where to find water: "One thing White Eyes never learned – to detect the presence of water underground. Many perished, when by digging two or three feet they could have obtained water."[10] This knowledge also allowed the Apaches to pollute obvious water sources without putting their own survival at risk. They also used the higher elevations in the mountains to watch for, and monitor the progress of, any enemies or targets in the vicinity.

Furthermore, Chiricahua Apaches were able to use the terrain for concealment prior to an ambush, often being able to remain undetected until the enemy was at point-blank range. The attack site would also have been

10   Kaywaykla in Ball (note 32) p.74. See also, Bourke, (note 41) pp.36–37 and Opler, (note 18), p.348.

D   VICTORIO DIRECTING ATTACK UPON CONLINE

On April 5, 1880, Lt. John Conline was attacked in the lower reaches of Hembrillo Canyon by Apaches led by Victorio. Conline had some warning of the attack, having deployed advance guards. However, he positioned his skirmish line poorly. This allowed the Apaches to infiltrate through rough terrain to his front. They also used a shallow arroyo to occupy positions above Conline's left flank. Finally, Conline failed to spot the danger of the dry arroyo running down Hembrillo Canyon. The Apaches used this to infiltrate around Conline's right flank to attack his skirmish line and horse herd from the rear. Conline was only saved from disaster by the onset of night, when the Apaches chose to break off the attack. Conline reported that:

> Victorio was heard giving orders in Apache to Chavanaw, one of his chiefs, 'to turn my right flank.'
> He was at the time in the rear of his line, and about 500 yards from us. Chavanaw was then opposite
> our right flank. Jose Carillo, one of the trailers with me, who speaks the Apache language and
> personally knows Victorio, reported this to me.

This plate shows the early stage of the attack, just as Victorio spotted the opportunity offered by the unguarded arroyo. Victorio (**1**) crouched on a bastion of the northern side of Hembrillo Canyon shouting instructions to one of his lieutenants, Chavanaw (**2**), to deploy some of the warriors below (**3**) to work their way around Conline's right flank (**4**) along the arroyo (**5**) to attack both the skirmish line (**6**) from the rear and to bring the horse herd and guards (**7**) under attack. Victorio is placed in this position as the archeology survey found a .44-40 cartridge suggesting that an Apache at that spot was carrying a Winchester 1873 repeating rifle/carbine.

Other warriors (**8**) have already worked their way forward through the rocky/bushy terrain to engage the 9th Cavalry's skirmish line from the front. Some warriors have managed to work their way to within 30–50 yards of Conline's men. Other warriors have ascended a very shallow arroyo (**9**) to occupy positions higher than the skirmish line. All are following the Apache dictum of exerting maximum pressure for minimal risk.

The inset shows some of the Apaches who worked their way behind Conline via the arroyo. We know they were armed with bows and arrows in addition to their modern rifles as archeological evidence shows that arrows were launched at the horse herd from the direction of the arroyo. By 1880, it would be very unusual for Apache warriors to be using the bow as their primary weapon of choice.

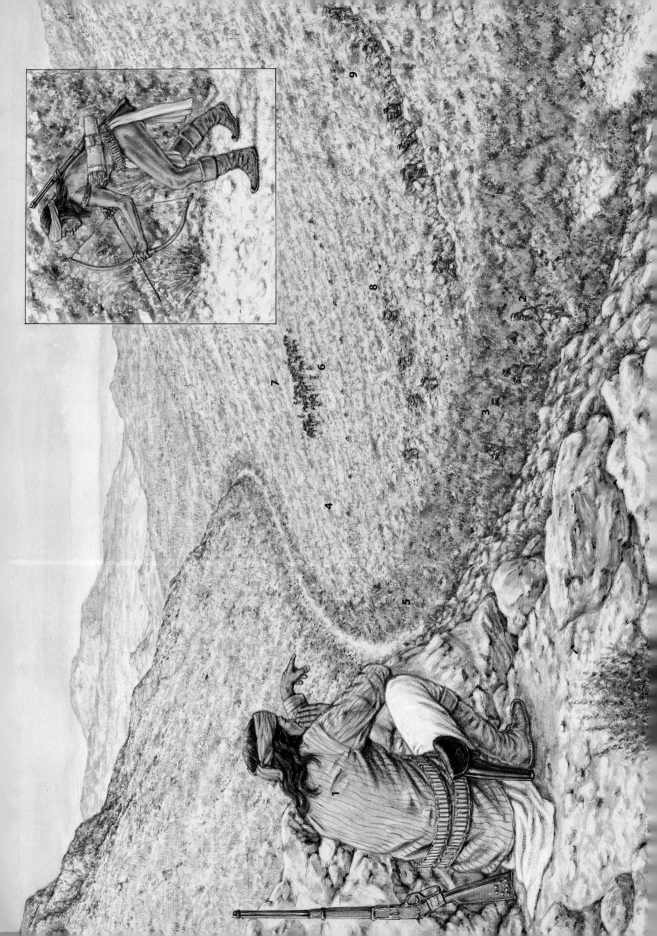

The eastern slopes of the San Mateo Mountains on the road into Nogal Canyon. Although high up in the San Mateos, this point is still a good way below the summit. Nevertheless, one can see the line of the Rio Grande, indicated by the dark line running almost horizontally across the photo (approximately 25km away as the crow flies), the Fra Cristobal Mountains (approx. 30km), the northern end of the San Andres Mountains (approx. 96km) and, at the maximum horizon with a tiny white cloud hovering at the peak, the Sierra Blanca (approx. 165km). Nobody is suggesting that the Apaches could determine targets at many of these distances, but even a small plume of dust raised by a cavalry patrol or wagon train could be detected from quite far away. (Author's photo)

chosen so as to allow the Apaches a safe and rapid retreat if the ambush failed. If the attack was successful, the Apaches could then use the terrain to infiltrate towards and around the survivors with the minimum risk to themselves. When Kaywaykla described the ambush of two groups of Mexican militia in the Candelaria Mountains in November 1879 he noted the fact that the Apaches' horses were hidden nearby to facilitate a quick withdrawal should the ambush fail.

Moreover, lookouts were stationed on the surrounding heights to make sure that the ambush was not surprised by a previously undetected force. Finally, the terrain was used in such a way as to manipulate the militiamen into reacting to the opening move of the ambush in exactly the way the Apaches wanted.[11] The basic principle was to always have at least one exit strategy from any camp, route march, ambush or attack while on campaign.

Another point that becomes very clear when visiting the sites of Chiricahua Apache ambushes is how little terrain was needed to spring the most deadly of ambushes. Thus, choosing to ambush targets in less obviously dangerous terrain was a key technique utilized by the Chiricahua Apaches. When Geronimo agreed to surrender to General Nelson A. Miles in September 1886, the US troops escorting Geronimo and his followers out of Mexico were shadowed by a large force of Mexican soldiers. Placing his forces between the Mexicans and the Apaches, the US commander Captain Henry Lawton entered into negotiations but received news from Geronimo and Naiche that if the two forces came to blows[12] they would support the

---

[11] For a detailed analysis of this ambush see Watt, *Apache Tactics*, Osprey Publishing (2012), pp. 28 & 30–31.

[12] This is not as strange as it might seem, as feelings were still running quite high in the US Army over the death of Captain Emmet Crawford who was killed by Chihuahuan state militia in January 1886 when leading Apache scouts in Mexico. Many fellow officers, including Crawford's second in command, Lt. Marion P. Maus, believed that the death was not accidental. Crawford's Apache scouts, who included the Chiricahua leader Chatto, killed four of the Mexican troops in retaliation.

US Army by circling round and attacking the Mexican troops from the rear. When Lawton realized the Mexicans did not intend to attack he sent his medical officer, Leonard Wood, with a message that the US troops would protect the Chiricahua Apaches. Finding that the Chiricahuas had moved their camp he set out in pursuit: "While following them up, one or two of the hostiles jumped up from behind a boulder along the trail, where they had evidently been lying as a rear guard. They joined me and trotted on. They were so well covered up that I did not see them until well on them. They could easily have shot me." (Wood, 1970, p.106.)

Plainly Geronimo and Naiche had no intention of placing blind trust in anybody and had left these warriors behind to make sure no treachery was planned. To Wood it was quite clear that had he been considered an enemy he would have been a dead man. His great relief that the Apaches no longer considered themselves at war with the US Army is clearly evident.

When threatened, Chiricahua Apaches could move large distances in a surprising short amount of time, often moving at night and using the stars for navigation. It was routine to agree a rendezvous point should the group be attacked and forced to scatter. Even when they had reconvened, the group would often set up a false camp and move on a few miles before setting up their real camp.

The role of women

The role of Chiricahua women on campaign was equally important as that of the men. Their logistical support for the warriors was an essential component of the Chiricahua Apaches' ability to engage in periods of prolonged conflict such as they faced from the 1860s onwards. As we have seen, the women were not only responsible for bringing up children but played a key role in reinforcing lessons about how to achieve warrior status. They gathered, prepared and stored food, fashioned footwear and made clothes. It has been argued that their detailed knowledge of natural food resources made Chiricahua Apache women better placed than the warriors to survive on their own for long periods of time.

The clearest example of this was the experience of Kaywaykla's sister and grandmother[13] who were captured at Tres Castillos on October 14, 1880. They were eventually sent to Mexico City and sold as slaves to a local landowner along with three other Chiricahua women. According to Kaywaykla's account of what his grandmother told him, she waited five winters before making an escape attempt. They managed to escape in the winter of 1885–86 and walked all the way from Mexico City to Canada Alamosa, the village nearest to their old reservation at Ojo Caliente, taking over three months to complete the journey. Once they reached their homeland they could rely upon caches scattered around for just such an eventuality. In the Florida Mountains, they found a cache left by Victorio in 1879–80. The bolts of calico had been damaged by mice but they were able to salvage enough to make new clothing.

Lozen was not the only woman seen to be vested with "power." Kaywaykla's grandmother was seen to have power over healing wounds and

---

[13] Kaywaykla refers to Nana and his wife as 'grandfather' and 'grandmother' and though they acted in the manner in which many Europeans would recognize they were actually grand uncle and aunt to Kaywaykla.

his mother was seen to have the power of avoiding battle injuries. This perhaps explains why Kaywaykla was so often instructed by his grandmother, as his mother accompanied his father during the fight for their reservation at Ojo Caliente in the late 1870s. Significantly, when his father was killed, Kaywaykla's mother had not been with her husband. It appears to have been accepted custom that during prolonged periods of warfare some Chiricahua women accompanied their husbands and, along with the *dikohe*, helped with the feeding and repairing of clothing, etc. However, it was unusual for women to take part in any deliberate fighting and in that respect Victorio's sister Lozen was very unusual.

Nevertheless, women could be caught up in hostilities. They could be used as decoys to lure targets into an ambush or they could be caught up in the fighting and killed. Apache warriors did not seem to hesitate to kill women and children if they thought it necessary. In early May 1880, warriors led by Victorio killed a number of Western Apaches, including women and children, as part of an ongoing feud which dated back to 1877 when the Chihennes were removed to San Carlos. In return, Western Apache scouts inflicted heavy casualties upon Victorio's following when they ambushed his camp in the

 MCEVERS RANCH, SEPTEMBER 1879

The Apaches staged their ambush close to McEvers Ranch to lull the posse into thinking that they were about to attack unsuspecting warriors besieging the ranch. If the ambush failed and the Apaches needed to retreat, Victorio could also signal the warriors picketing the ranch to withdraw.

For the attack, Victorio would have placed himself in a strategic command position (**1**). From this point he could shout commands to his warriors at (**2**) and (**3**) and communicate with his men stationed at (**4**), (**5**) and (**6**) using mirror signals or waved blankets. These signals would be arranged before deployment. From this point Victorio could also keep an eye on the men attacking McEver's Ranch to make sure that nothing unexpected occurred from that direction.

The warriors at (**2**) probably opened fire first, stopping the posse in its tracks by firing down the straight part of the road at almost point-blank range. They would have aimed for horses first and men second. They would also have been the best shots in the group. Seconds after them, the next group of warriors (**3**) would have opened fire into the mass of confused men and wounded horses. Another group of warriors (**4**) would be responsible for closing the door of the trap, opening fire from behind the ambushed men. Again, these warriors would have been selected on the basis of their good marksmanship.

A warrior or two would have been stationed higher up (**5**) at the back of (**4**) to warn of any reinforcements who might realize what had happened and try to attack the warriors at (**4**) from the rear and also threaten the flank of the Apaches stationed along (**3**).

The ambushed party would have been prevented from retreating away from the main Apache ambush positions at (**2**), (**3**) and (**4**) by two or three older warriors, armed with Springfield rifles, who kept up a harassing fire from the only apparent direction of escape (**6**). Victorio would also have needed advance warning of the approach of the Hillsboro men and news of their enemies could be easily signaled by mirror from this point. This position also dominated the marshy area where the Hillsboro survivors took refuge.

It should also be noted that while (**2**), (**3**), (**4**), (**5**) and (**6**) were at close range and virtually surrounded the target, the chances of "friendly fire" were minimized as all of the Apache positions were several feet above their targets and so all of the Apaches aimed their fire downwards towards (**7**) and (**8**).

Most of the casualties, including horses, were inflicted in the opening volleys of the ambush (**7**). The survivors were forced into the marshy area to take cover (**8**) and were kept pinned down for approximately ten hours. A local historian states that ten men were killed and seven survivors managed to hold out.

The ever-cautious Apaches would have taken precautions to allow a quick flight should the ambush fail. The dead side of the ridge would have provided an ideal spot where a few apprentice warriors could hold the horses ready for an immediate retreat should that prove necessary (**9**).

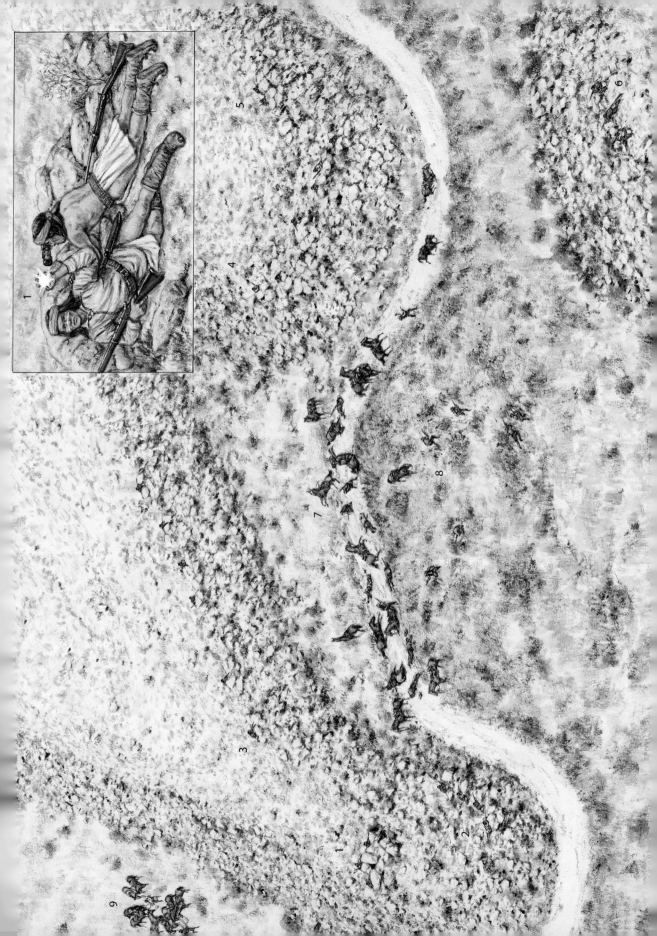

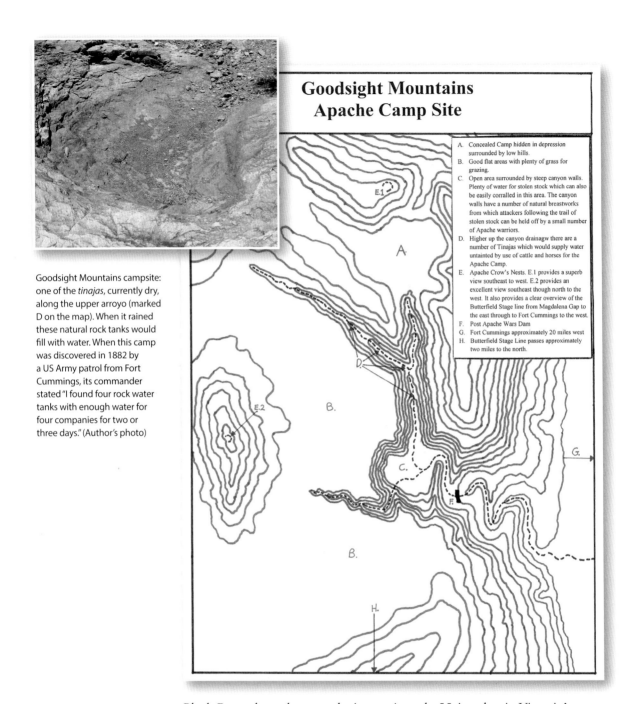

Goodsight Mountains campsite: one of the *tinajas*, currently dry, along the upper arroyo (marked D on the map). When it rained these natural rock tanks would fill with water. When this camp was discovered in 1882 by a US Army patrol from Fort Cummings, its commander stated "I found four rock water tanks with enough water for four companies for two or three days." (Author's photo)

Goodsight Mountains Apache Camp Site

A. Concealed Camp hidden in depression surrounded by low hills.
B. Good flat areas with plenty of grass for grazing.
C. Open area surrounded by steep canyon walls. Plenty of water for stolen stock which can also be easily corralled in this area. The canyon walls have a number of natural breastworks from which attackers following the trail of stolen stock can be held off by a small number of Apache warriors.
D. Higher up the canyon drainagw there are a number of Tinajas which would supply water untainted by use of cattle and horses for the Apache Camp.
E. Apache Crow's Nests. E.1 provides a superb view southeast to west. E.2 provides an excellent view southeast though north to the west. It also provides a clear overview of the Butterfield Stage line from Magdalena Gap to the east through to Fort Cummings to the west.
F. Post Apache Wars Dam
G. Fort Cummings approximately 20 miles west
H. Butterfield Stage Line passes approximately two miles to the north.

Black Range later that month. Approximately 55 Apaches in Victorio's camp were killed and most were women and children. In 1885, Ulzana's warriors killed approximately 20 Western Apaches including 11 women and four children. It was believed that these killings had taken place as retaliation for Western Apaches serving as scouts against the Chiricahua Apaches. When Victorio's camp was attacked in the Cuchillo Negro Mountains on September 29, 1879 he lost two warriors and a woman to Apache scouts who spearheaded the attack. Chiricahua Apache girls were, therefore, given hard physical training as, given the unforgiving nature of Apache warfare, they could not necessarily expect different treatment from the warriors if caught and thus had to be able to move over the same rough terrain to escape any attack.

Goodsight Mountains campsite: shot looking down into the central area where horses, mules and cattle could be corralled under guard (point C on the map). (Author's photo)

As a result, while generally subordinate to the warriors, experienced women would sometimes be called upon to contribute to councils held by the warriors.

The choice of campsites

Throughout the 1860s to 1880s, US Army officers noted that the Chiricahua Apaches would carefully select their campsites for both ease of defence and ease of exit should they be overwhelmed. If there was not enough natural cover, small breastworks were sometimes constructed to enhance the defences of a campsite. While the Chiricahua Apaches were nomadic, they also had a number of favorite camping spots. The Apaches would try to ensure that they remained undiscovered by the enemy. However, if the camp was discovered it would be well fortified and difficult to surround.

Other semi-permanent locations would be staging points on well-traveled raiding and trade routes. However, as raiding was central to Chiricahua Apache culture, every effort would be made to keep such locations secret. One such example, which was used for a number of years as a staging post for Chiricahua Apache raiding and war parties, was located in the Goodsight Mountains in southern New Mexico. This site remained undiscovered until it was stumbled upon by a routine army patrol from Fort Cumings in 1882. By that time, the Chiricahua Apaches had ceased to use the site as a staging post when moving stolen cattle and horses from Mexico to sell in the USA. The site

Goodsight Mountains campsite: the view from the "crow's nest" at E2. The distinctive flat-topped mesa on the horizon is known as Massacre Peak. It was so named as in October 1879 a train of 12 Mexican *carretas* (carts) was wiped out by Chihenne Apaches in the shadow of this mesa. The stage road passed this mesa to the left of the photo and went across the flat ground moving down towards the left side of the photograph, above the cloud shadow. Massacre Peak is approximately 17 miles away as the crow flies. On a day such as this a dust cloud would be clearly detected once its source had passed the mesa. (Author's photo)

Goodsight Mountains campsite: "crow's nest" at E2. (Author's photo)

was in close proximity to where the road between La Mesilla and Old Fort Cummings passed through the Goodsight Mountains. In September 1880, and again in January 1881, travellers, some on stagecoaches, were waylaid and killed by Apaches whose camp was hidden about two miles from the road.

This camp was well chosen (see diagram on pp. 42). Even when quite close to the site it did not look as if there could be a camp in the vicinity. It was surrounded by low ridges that gave a good all-round perspective of the surrounding country, yet these ridges were not high and rugged enough to suggest to any foes that they might be worth investigating as a possible campsite. There was a natural opening in a well-hidden canyon where horses, mules and cattle could be corralled with access to plenty of water. In the higher reaches of the canyon there were at least four *tinajas*, or natural rock tanks, which would hold fresh water for some time after any rainfall. These tanks could not be reached by the corralled livestock, so would provide

Goodsight Mountains campsite: view down the canyon from the western edge of Point C. Any pursuit of a trail would come up the canyon towards the photographer. Good cover can be seen on either side of the canyon for Chiricahua riflemen to use. (Author's photo)

good water for the Apache camp placed in a shallow depression at the top of one of one of the canyon branches. If the Apaches stayed there for more than a fleeting instance there were a couple of areas of good grass they could use to feed their animals, and alert Apache guards could easily prevent their animals from straying out to where they might attract the attention of their enemies.

There were a couple of what could be described as small crow's nests built on top of the ridges. These offered an excellent overview of the surrounding countryside. One of them overlooked the stage road as it ran through the southern reaches of the Sierra Uvas, crossed the open ground and entered the Goodsight Mountains. The dust raised by an approaching wagon or stagecoach would give ample warning should the Apaches wish to ambush such a target. Today it takes about 15 minutes to walk from the lookout to the camp, and a fit Chiricahua lookout would be able to raise the alarm in a considerably shorter time. Of course the lookout, armed with a mirror, could summon his compatriots so as the potential target could be evaluated. This would leave plenty of time to lay an ambush if the odds looked favorable.

Goodsight Mountains campsite: if under continued attack, the Apaches could fall back from one outcrop of rock to another. This photo is taken from the southern mid edge of Point C on the map. The Apaches never had to mount such a defence, as this campsite was not found until after they had ceased to use the location. (Author's photo)

Finally, there was no need to construct breastworks, as, should the Apaches be trailed to the canyon by their enemies, there was ample natural cover by which a rearguard of warriors could fall back from position to position up the canyon, thereby giving the rest of the Apaches time to flee.

This site was an ideal camp from the Apache point of view as it was not discovered until after they had virtually ceased to operate in this area of New Mexico. Thus, while it was very well defended, the intention was that they should not have to defend such a location in the first place.

Smoke and mirrors: long-range communication

In an attempt to coordinate their actions, Chiricahua Apaches on campaign used various techniques to communicate with each other over long distances. They mainly used smoke signals (by day), signal fires (by night) and mirrors for this purpose. To understand this means of communicating, we must first divest ourselves of the old Hollywood image of the grizzled old army scout seeing smoke signals and reading off a detailed plan of action. The use of smoke and fire signals was much less complicated, as the Chiricahuas knew their limitations and used such media to convey very simple messages.

For example, during the late 1870s, an Apache leader might decide that he was going to use the Goodsight Mountains camp to move some stolen

Steins Peak, with the remains of the Steins Peak stagecoach station in the foreground. There were regular sightings of signal fires on the top of this mountain during the Apache Wars. The canyon through which the stage road passed is known as Doubtful Canyon, as it was such a popular site for ambushes during the Apache Wars. One of the reasons this would be a popular spot for signal fires is that the peak is clearly recognizable from a distance. (Author's photo)

cattle and horses from Mexico up to the Mescalero reservation to sell for guns and ammunition. However, he would have known that the US Army had a string of piquets and patrols looking for signs of hostile Apaches crossing the border. The trail of a herd of stolen stock would be difficult, if not impossible, to hide from such patrols. Therefore, the leader would divide his warriors into two groups. The first group would be made up of the younger warriors and a few senior warriors. They would be instructed to move into the USA ahead of the second group of older warriors who were tasked with driving the herd. The task of the first group was to attract the US Army's attention and draw them away from the area through which the leader wished to drive his plunder. The use of pre-arranged smoke and/or fire signals was the means by which the second group of Apaches was informed that the attempt to decoy the US Army away from their intended path had been successful. This was possible because of the Apaches' thorough knowledge of the topography of their land. The plan might be coordinated something like this:

The whole group crosses the border and camps at the southern end of the Florida Mountains.

On day one, the first group moves north through, or around, Cooke's Range with instructions to cut the telegraph line between Silver City and La Mesilla and leave an obvious trail to follow. They are instructed to detach a warrior to a designated point at the southern end of the Black Range and light one fire if successful and two fires if unsuccessful in two days' time.

The second group sends out a scout to the top of Cooke's Range to watch for the signal fires. He then replicates the signal – one fire for success, etc.

The second group of Apaches also sends a man to the top of the Florida Mountains to watch for the signal from Cooke's Range.

On day three, one fire is seen from the Black Range by the lookout on Cooke's Range and his corresponding signal fire is seen by the man on the

Florida Mountains. He makes his way down to the camp and the second group now knows it is safe to pass on from the Floridas across to the Goodsight Mountain camp.

If two fires were seen, then the leader of the second group had to act independently and try to make his way through to the Mescalero Reservation. However, having a scout deployed on Cooke's Range and on top of the Florida Mountains would also give him a good idea of any US Army detachments or other potential enemies still in the area. Smoke signals could be deployed in the same way during daylight.

There was also another use for such signals. Fires and smoke signals could be used to deliberately send enemies in the wrong direction. This took advantage of the knowledge that at least some of their opponents knew that the Chiricahuas would use such signals, and would investigate the area. There was at least one incident of signal fires being seen on Steins Peak in mid-January 1881 when Chiricahua Apache raiders appeared to be active far to the east of that point in New Mexico. This caused immediate speculation in the local press and would have provided the US Army with additional intelligence as to potential Apache activity. The army was forced to divert their already scarce resources to check these sightings, taking them away from the attacks in New Mexico. However, there were no attacks reported in the Steins Peak area. It is possible that there was another group of Apaches operating in, or at least passing through, the Stein's Peak area who were letting their compatriots in the mountains of New Mexico know that they had reached that point safely. It is equally possible that a couple of warriors were simply detached to that point to provide an additional distraction. The modern phrase "smoke and mirrors" to indicate deception and confusion is particularly apt when referring to this use of signals by the Apaches.

The Chiricahua Apaches were also quick to realize the potential for using the telegraph – their enemies' long-range communications technology – to their advantage. They could deliberately cut telegraph lines to attract attention to a specific spot. This would either be done to tempt the army into a pursuit of the Apaches or to distract their attention away from where the Apaches intended to strike.

A much cleverer device was designed to knock out communications and hamper the ability of the army to coordinate its scattered forces against the Apaches. The line would still be cut, but the cut ends were fastened together using rawhide either at the top of a pole or where the line passed through some trees. The failure of the telegraph would be quickly detected but the repair teams would have to check every pole and natural obstruction before the link could be repaired. By such time, the news that Chiricahua Apaches were in a specific area would be obsolete. However, they would not always have left the area. One telegraph repair party of four soldiers was surprised and wiped out by Juh's warriors on October 2, 1881 as the Apaches were making for Mexico after leaving the San Carlos Reservation. The party had been sent out to find the break in the line made by the Chiricahuas earlier in the day.

Mirrors were probably used for much shorter-range communication than signal fires. Kaywaykla recalls that mirrors were utilized as part of coordinating the ambush of Mexican militia in the Candelaria Mountains. Here mirrors were used by the group of Apaches tasked with blocking any attempt by the Mexicans to flee back down the canyon, to alert the other Apaches that all of the Mexicans had entered the ambush zone and to

Replica Springfield 45/55 carbine bullet (left) and Springfield 45/70 rifle round (right). Both could be used by a carbine or rifle but the difference in size, evident in this photograph, meant that a rifle round loaded into a carbine would have a vicious recoil. (Author's photo)

commence firing (see Elite 119; *Apache Tactics 1830–86* by the same author, pp.30–31) They were usually carried on a thong around a warrior's neck. The Chiricahuas also used a system of rocks or twigs that would be laid out in such a way as to appear innocuous to an ignorant observer but which could be seen and understood by fellow Apaches.

Illicit trade networks

During a prolonged campaign, the main challenge for the Chiricahua Apaches was the maintenance of a secure supply of guns and ammunition. Weapons and ammunition could be picked up during fighting where they could be taken from, for example, dead soldiers, prospectors or ranchers. There were also several instances when Apaches, led by Victorio and Nana, captured mules carrying reserve ammunition packs belonging to US Army detachments. The occasional cavalry courier would yield up a Springfield carbine, a Colt revolver and between 50 and 100 rounds of ammunition. There were also a few instances when small detachments of troops were ambushed and forced to withdraw, allowing the Apaches to loot the bodies for weapons and ammunition. This would supply cartridges that would fit either the Springfield rifle or carbine, though if the rifle round was fired from the carbine the recoil was apparently quite brutal, as the carbine round had 55 grains of powder whereas the rifle round had 70 grains (see photo).

 SOLDIER HILL AMBUSH, 19 DECEMBER 1885

A detachment from Company C, 8th Cavalry, was ambushed by Apaches led by Josanie, also known as Ulzana, at what came to be known as Soldier Hill in commemoration of this event. The Apaches took positions above the wagon road as it climbed obliquely up a ridge before turning to the right as it made the ridge, and opened fire at point-blank range. Five men were killed, including Surgeon Maddox who, after being hit for the first time, managed to dismount before being killed by a shot to the head. Two other men, including Lt. De Rosey C. Cabell, were wounded. Interestingly, their Navajo scouts had refused to set out that morning as they thought that the Apaches were in the vicinity and knew the latter would not have any qualms about killing Indian scouts. Lt. Samuel W. Fountain, commanding the detachment, missed the ambush because he had remained behind to try to encourage his scouts to rejoin the expedition.

This plate shows an Apache warrior (**1**) armed with a Springfield carbine who has moved a small flat boulder into a position that will help make his first shot count. He has also ensured that his target is only yards away on the road immediately below him. The Apache warrior to his right (**2**) has spotted the dismounted Surgeon Maddox and shoots him dead with a shot to the head (**3**). Another warrior (**4**) reaches for a cartridge case for his Remington rifle in his ammunition belt while yet another (**5**) blasts away with his Winchester repeating rifle into the surprised 8th Cavalry company. One warrior (**6**), having just fired his Springfield rifle, reaches to where he has placed a handful of cartridges which are positioned to help speed up his reloading. A group of warriors (**7**), stationed slightly above where the trail turns and reaches the top of the ridge, fire down the length of the column. The attack caused a confused mass of shot or panicking horses (**8**) and soldier casualties. Those not hit desperately tried to control their horses (if they have not already had their mounts shot from under them) or free their weapons. One suspects that the column was particularly thrown not only by the closeness of the volley but also by the fact that one of their number sent on ahead of them as a courier had passed through the ambush point without being attacked and was still close enough to hear the gunfire when the ambush was sprung. The Apaches had clearly remained hidden and allowed the man to pass unmolested.

The old church at Janos, Chihuahua, Mexico, which dates back to the Apache Wars period. Note the heavy and barred windows, most of which are far above ground level. While places such as Janos, Casas Grandes and Galeana were known for their lively trade with the Apaches, hostilities could erupt with no warning. Therefore, this place of worship would also become a place of refuge which the Apaches would be reluctant to assault. One method of catching the Apaches off guard was to let them get drunk in a tavern before shutting the doors and windows and throwing in a "chili bomb." This was a simple bag stuffed with dried and powdered pepper leaves mixed in with loose gunpowder and lit with a rudimentary fuse. The effect was similar to the effect of modern pepper spray and would leave the inebriated Apaches as easy prey. However, Apache testimony states that they themselves used such a bomb on a small village church where Mexican villagers had taken refuge. They did not use a fuse but dropped it through a hole in the roof onto an open fire below. In 2013, in India, a chili grenade, a sophisticated version of the above device, was judged fit for use to help flush out terrorists from buildings. (Author's photos)

It should come as no surprise that the archeological surveys of two of Victorio's battlefields show that a number of his warriors were armed with these weapons.

The US Army in the Southwest does not appear to have armed itself with repeating rifles, though it is possible that the occasional Spencer repeating rifle may have got into the hands of the Apaches from the US Army in the 1860s. From the 1870s, the Apaches appeared to be quite well armed with lever-action repeating rifles and carbines such as the Winchester. These had to be obtained from somewhere, and again one source would be citizens (ranchers, freighters, prospectors, herders, etc.) armed with such weapons. It was rare for the Apaches to directly attack buildings, but occasionally a general store or ranch building might be ransacked and a fair haul of weapons and ammunition taken. However, these sources would not provide a regular supply of modern weapons.

The hamlet of Canada Alamosa, now called Monticello, in New Mexico. The peaks of the San Mateo Mountains can be seen in the background. The hamlet maintained very good relations with the Chihenne Apaches and trading was said to occur in the cottonwood groves just outside the village. This relationship was widely condemned by the local press and just before trade between the two ended an ominous letter, probably from one of the more recent American settlers, was published in one of the local newspapers: "We have made up our minds that the cottonwoods in this vicinity shall bear fruit if there are any midnight meetings between Victorio's men and some of the persons of this town." (Author's photo)

The main sources of such weapons and ammunition were illicit trade networks on both sides of the border. These networks flourished for as long as state, or even federal, government did not exercise control. South of the border, the 1860s to 1880s was a period of turmoil with both Chihuahua and Sonora, which the central Mexican authorities were unable to control very effectively, riven by internal state rivalries. Occasionally, the Mexican Federal Army intervened in such conflicts and as a result sometimes ended up taking the field against hostile Apaches. However, this did not appear to have been a part of a systematic national policy. The Mexican state troops could be very effective and were sometimes well armed with Remington rifles, carbines, and revolvers, but these were not consistently held in the field and were organized on an almost feudal basis around the patronage of very rich local landowners.

In this state of anarchy, local communities did the best they could to survive, and a cycle of hostilities and trade relations with Chiricahua Apaches gave the Apaches a clear source of illegal arms and ammunition. Trading was a risky venture, though, as towns might also take advantage of the periodic bounties offered for Apache scalps by the state governments of Chihuahua and Sonora. Such a relationship could be termed a trade/hate relationship and the change from trade to hate could occur without warning. The usual ploy the townspeople would use was to have a big siesta after trading with the Chiricahuas had been concluded. They would then get the Apaches drunk and bludgeon them to death while they were helpless. Equally, if the Chiricahua Apaches realized that they had a clear advantage over their trading partners, then these traders might count themselves very fortunate to emerge from the experience alive but penniless. Apaches and Mexicans thoroughly distrusted, even loathed, each other. When circumstances were right for either side both the Mexicans and the Apaches could be utterly merciless. The problem for the Mexican townships living in a state of anarchy was that trade with the Apaches had clear economic benefits, and the Apaches could see the advantages as well. However, trading with Mexican townships was one of the most potentially dangerous activities for Chiricahua Apache warriors and their families. The danger was so great that leaders such as Victorio and Mangus forbade their

The impromptu grave marker of two miners killed by Apaches a short distance outside a small mining settlement in New Mexico called Chloride. (Photo by J. R. Absher)

men to get drunk when trading with these towns and to be on their guard at all times. Not all Chiricahua leaders were so cautious and both Geronimo and Juh had a number of narrow escapes while trading and both were sometimes criticized by other Chiricahuas for the losses incurred during such episodes.

That said, the Chihenne Apaches had good relationships with a couple of Mexican villages (Las Palomas and particularly Canada Alamosa) in the US near their strongholds in the northern Black Range and San Mateo Mountains. They also had good relations with a few Mexican ranchers in the same area. These relationships were occasionally fraught with violence but seemed to be more cordial than most relations between the Apaches and Mexicans south of the border, to the extent that it was rumored that wounded Apaches were sometimes sheltered by these communities and there was regular trading for guns and ammunition.

Another source of probably small amounts of munitions was the many isolated Mexican sheep herders scattered across Apacheria. The dealings with them amounted to a small-scale Apache protection racket – it would take

The probable area of the McEver's Ranch ambush site where, in September 1879, Victorio and some of his warriors attacked a posse from the mining town of Hillsboro, New Mexico (see Plate E for detail). Victorio could try to coordinate his different squads from just behind and above the immediate foreground of the photo, but he was also relying upon leaders of each squad to be able to direct their own element of this ambush and, if things went wrong, use their initiative to extricate themselves as quickly as possible. (Author's photo)

a very brave shepherd to refuse to trade with a group of Apaches if they turned up at his camp. These trades were more likely to provide the Chiricahuas with food than guns, but a small number could still be garnered.

Modern rifles and ammunition would not necessarily always be available in Mexican towns. More reliable suppliers were US Hispanic communities and Anglo-American traders, including reservation agents and employees, in the USA. However, relations with the Hispanic communities, ranchers and shepherds in New Mexico broke down in 1880. This can be linked to an increase in Anglo-American settlers, who put pressure on their neighbors to

Opposite view of the probable location of the McEvers Ranch ambush site from the one shown in the previous photograph. A pickup truck is shown for scale. (Author's photo)

cease such trading or suffer the consequences. The irony is that one of the early Anglo-Americans to arrive in the area, who had such a good relationship with the Chihenne that he was suspected of trading illicit goods with them, was also the first to lead the charge against such activities. Unfortunately, when relations started to go sour, the Apaches killed a large number of Hispanic sheepherders in retaliation in April and May of 1880.

The Apaches also garnered munitions from the miners and prospectors who increasingly penetrated Apacheria in search of silver and gold. Even today the Southwest of the USA is awash with stories of lost mines dating back to the Spanish settlement. What is true is that there were a number of substantial silver discoveries in the region in the 1870s and 1880s. The conflict between prospectors and Chiricahua Apaches was well-known enough to provide the backdrop to one of Sherlock Holmes' investigations, *The Adventure of the Noble Batchelor*, published in 1892. The nature of their work made prospectors very vulnerable to hostile Chiricahua Apaches as they tended to act alone or in very small groups – the smaller the group, the larger the share in whatever gold or silver deposits discovered. They might be very well armed but their low numbers worked against them. At least one relatively well-connected Englishman, Walter Guy Barnes, disappeared in southern New Mexico in 1879 after outfitting himself for prospecting, and even enquiries prompted by the British Minister to the USA found no trace of his fate.

The notoriously lax and corrupt administration of Apache reservations by agents and their employees, who were appointed by the Department of the Interior through the Office of Indian Affairs, gave the Chiricahua Apaches a major source of munitions. Arms and ammunition could be issued to Apaches for hunting with no concern for how they might utilize such weapons. Furthermore, the way the reservations were run also allowed unscrupulous Anglo-American traders and ranchers to trade alcohol and munitions for plunder taken in both the USA and Mexico, with no questions asked. Again, this was a hazardous venture for both parties, but the trade was more than lucrative enough for some individuals to take such risks.

Independent squad leader system

One of the key strengths of the Chiricahua Apaches on campaign has already been alluded to earlier; each individual warrior was capable of leadership or, more accurately, using their initiative while on campaign. Such an emphasis on trust during a warrior's training meant that a warrior entrusted with being at a certain place at a certain time, for example, to light a signal fire, could be trusted to do the task in hand.

The successes of major Chiricahua Apache leaders such as Cochise, Mangas Coloradas, Victorio, Juh and Nana were built upon having sub-leaders they could trust to carry out individual elements of their overall planning. This obedience was tempered by the warriors having the initiative to change the plan should it start to go wrong. This ability to immediately act on their own initiative if a circumstance changed was governed by the other key principle of their training – maximum damage for the minimum loss. No Apache leader would complain if his plan started to go wrong and his squad leaders spotted it and acted to avert disaster. Such a leader's success was often founded upon choosing the right warriors to lead each component of a plan and being able to trust their judgement as the plan was executed. If time allowed, a leader's plan would be discussed and analysed by his warriors. If the plan was accepted, or even if modified, it would be very rare for Chiricahua Apaches on campaign not to have discussed and agreed upon at least one alternative plan should what appeared to be an excellent plan suddenly go wrong. The warrior groups involved in attacks were usually small enough for every warrior to know each other by name and this gave the Chiricahua Apache guerrilla a huge tactical advantage in battle.

EXPERIENCE OF BATTLE

Patience and nerve were key attributes of the Chiricahua Apaches during combat. The two Chiricahua rearguards, mentioned earlier, who did not reveal their presence to Wood until he was at point-blank range are a good example of these attributes. In 1872, Fuller accompanied some Apaches on a hunting trip and observed that while American Indians were generally poor shots, Apaches were "more certain shots, since they will not fire until almost upon the object." (Fuller in Cozzens, 2005, p.467.) The same techniques were clearly utilized in warfare and their first shot was liable to be quite accurate, due to the combination of close range and the fact that the Apaches preferred to use a rock or a forked stick to steady their aim. The point that it was standard practice for the Chiricahuas to aim at the horse rather than the rider with their first shot possibly accounts for quite low human fatalities during ambushes. If one reads US Army reports they often comment upon the low or non-existent human casualties but fail to realize the significance of losing high numbers of horses. The reason for this practice was that, at minimum, the Apaches required that an ambush should cripple the ability of their foe to maintain any pursuit of the attacking party.

If during a Chiricahua ambush or attack one of the warriors got into difficulties, for example by being wounded or isolated, then he would call out

Close-up photo of the small cave used by the two trapped Apache warriors at Tres Castillos. It has just enough room for two men to lie down in and any attacker would find it difficult to approach without coming under the fire of the warriors. (Author's photo)

to his nearest compatriots by name and they would be obliged to return to the fight to help extricate him. Obviously, if all was lost then the warrior might still be killed. However, as long as those named had done everything to try to help the stricken fighter then they would not be censured. Whether blamed or not, familial relationships would mean that the loss would be keenly felt by those who had tried but failed to rescue the warrior. Apparently, the Chihenne leader known as "Loco" got his Mexican name after he stopped and rescued a comrade who called out for his aid when their raiding party was ambushed by Mexicans in the 1840s.

A cornered Chiricahua was very rare, as the warriors would always enter battle with an exit strategy. However, no such plan can be perfect and occasionally warriors would be trapped. When this happened, a very dangerous situation was created. In this type of warfare the Apache warrior could expect little mercy and with no other option: "When a Chiricahua is cornered and desperate and thinks the end has come, he tears off all his clothes but his loincloth, and he goes right into the thick of it. Sometimes he fights so hard that he gets away." (Opler, 1996, p.349.)

Given no other option, to come out fighting or at least refusing to surrender might be their only chance of survival. When Chihuahua state troopers cornered Victorio at Tres Castillos, two warriors were trapped in a very small cave and it took the Mexican troops a couple of hours to finish them off. This was despite the troopers using Apache women captives to offer the men quarter. Their refusal to surrender makes sense on two grounds. Colonel Joaquin Terrazas, the Mexican commander, made a fortune out of the scalp bounty offered by the Chihuahua state government, then under the governorship of his cousin Luis Terrazas. Had the warriors surrendered, they

G **CHIRICAHUA APACHE WARRIOR, 1880s**

The Chiricahua Apache warrior of the 1880s would still have worn the practical breechclout and boots of his predecessors. However, while the headband was still very popular, European hats would also have been worn. Field-glasses and telescopes were still sought after (**1**).

An Apache warrior armed with a single-shot rifle/carbine would find a revolver a useful addition to his armory. It could be very easily fired on the move, so the rate of fire could be used by Apaches, moving swiftly from cover to cover, to give a false impression of their numbers (**2**). Breech-loading, single-shot and repeating rifles/carbines were prevalent, with muskets now only being found in the hands of adolescents. By the 1880s even such boys might be quite well armed with modern carbines, etc. Therefore, Springfield rifles and carbines were common (**4**). Remingtons were less prevalent but still present in some numbers (**3**). Winchester 1866 and 1873 rifles and carbines were also common (**6**). Sharps rifles were sometimes used by the Apaches (**5**). Sharps carbines and Henry and Spencer repeating rifles, rare in the 1860s, would have been less prevalent but were still being used in the 1870s and 1880s.

What must be noted is that the Apaches used a wide variety of weapons as they would pick up a large range of revolvers and rifles in trade and from the bodies of those they killed. Therefore, the weapons illustrated are merely the most common. The archeological surveys of the Hembrillo Canyon battles of April 5–7, 1880 provide a good idea of the variety of weapons carried by Apache warriors in 1880.

The one weapon the Apache did not appear to favor was the shotgun. In old age one warrior recorded that as apprentices he and a companion stole a couple of shotguns from Fort Cummings. When they handed them over to Mangus, the leader of their group, he tried them out but was knocked over by the recoil and was less than impressed by their accuracy. Mangus was furious and dismissed the shotgun as useless. While the use of shotguns cannot be completely ruled out, they were probably very rare. A rifle or carbine of similar weight to a shotgun could be used at various ranges, whereas the shotgun could only be used at very short range, limiting its usefulness.

would have been, at best, simply shot out of hand. The second reason is that had they managed to hold out until darkness, they might have been able to infiltrate the Mexican troops and escape out of the trap, as Terrazas' command was short of supplies and could not afford to linger. Also, less than a day later 30 warriors, who had been sent out to replenish ammunition stocks, returned to Tres Castillos.

In 1882, when the Sierra Madre Chiricahuas were moving those Chiricahua Apaches who had remained on the San Carlos reservation into Mexico, they were ambushed by Mexican troops under the command of Col. Lorenzo Garcia. The opening assault caught the main body, mainly made up of women and children, by surprise, and many were killed. The warriors in the rearguard intervened and made a stand by digging into an arroyo. A furious battle ensued with no quarter given. The warriors were clearly outnumbered by the Mexican soldiers but the manner in which the Apaches used the terrain and firepower to maximum effect prevented far higher casualties being sustained. The actions of a warrior known as Yahe-chul, or Fun, show how this could be done. Armed with a Springfield rifle and holding the bullets between his fingers, he charged towards the Mexicans three times, dodging back and forth to delay their advance. He was later described as running up and down the arroyo firing as he went, giving the impression that there were more warriors present than were actually there. Other warriors concealed themselves and one man was credited with killing five Mexican soldiers before his location was pinpointed and he was killed. An old woman also dashed out of the cover of the arroyo to recover a bag full of cartridges. The Apaches refused to give up and survivors managed to slip away after darkness fell. Nevertheless, the cost was heavy on both sides; the Chiricahuas lost approximately 12 warriors out of the 78 Apaches killed and a further 33 women and children were captured. In return, Garcia lost four officers and 19 other ranks killed and as many as 40 wounded.[14]

AFTER THE BATTLE

If Chiricahua Apaches held the ground after an ambush, then they would usually finish off any adult male wounded and prisoners. To save valuable ammunition, they often used rocks, clubs and rifle butts to break the skulls of the fallen to ensure that their enemies were truly dead. There was some mutilation of the bodies by lances. However, the regular accounts of mutilation may simply refer to the practice of making sure their enemies were dead. When Juh's warriors attacked a freight train on October 2, 1881, they thought they had killed all seven teamsters. One man survived as he feigned death after being shot through the leg. A warrior did roll him onto his front using the barrel of what was probably a Springfield rifle and then struck him a hefty blow using the butt of said rifle. However, a US Army detachment was in close pursuit and the Chiricahuas were disturbed and had to move on. One wonders whether the survivor would have been able to keep up his pretence had the Apaches not been forced to leave.

[14] For those interested in more detailed accounts of this battle I thoroughly commend first and foremost Bud Shapard's biography of Loco, Chapter 14. Sweeney, (2010), pp.222–229 and Robinson, (2000), Chapter 4 also give valuable detail about this particularly savage battle.

The Chiricahua Apaches also had a fearsome reputation for torturing some of their adult male prisoners after successful attacks. However, this practice appears to have been more prevalent in the 1860s when the Chiricahuas were trying to hold on to their homeland. At this time, it was clearly intended to send a psychological message to their enemies showing that their presence was unwelcome and could carry grave consequences. In the 1870s and 1880s, the Apaches were much more likely to be on the move to keep ahead of their enemies so would be less inclined to waste their time torturing prisoners. There is an account of a US citizen who escaped from a stagecoach being ransacked in Mexico in June 1881. He concluded that the Apaches must have got what they wanted and returned to the coach against the entreaties of the other passengers. He was later found tied to one of the wheels. However, he had not been tortured but simply dispatched with a single shot to the head. Equally, the same Chiricahuas spared a number of adult males in August 1881 near Monica Springs in New Mexico. The men were ex-reservation employees the warriors had known when they were on one of the Apache reservations in the early 1870s.

The Apaches used such summary executions as after an attack or ambush they would usually try to put as much distance between themselves and the site of the attack as possible in as short a period of time as was possible. Apaches mounted on good horses could sometimes cover between 60 and 80 miles in 24 hours. By the time pursuers got themselves organized their quarry could often be far beyond their reach. However, predictability being the cardinal sin of guerrilla warfare occasionally Chiricahua Apaches would stay in the area to catch out further targets who had assumed that the guerrillas would have departed.

Concluding comment

Emile Durkheim, one of the fathers of modern sociology, developed a concept of social solidarity which might help us understand the nature of the conflict between the Chiricahua Apaches and, particularly, the USA. The Chiricahua Apaches belonged to a small-scale, uncomplicated, in Durkheim's terms, "mechanical society." Social cohesion was supported by close family ties and a common identity such as "hunter" or "warrior." Durkheim, however, would term the USA an "organic society" where the identity and cohesion of individuals was based upon a much more abstract notion drawn from ideas promoted in the *Declaration of Independence* and the US Constitution, which were designed to form large-scale, complex nations. US citizens performed specific work such as "soldier," "merchant," "politician" or "teacher"; such diverse occupations were bound together under these abstract notions to produce a much larger-scale social cohesion.

The conflict between the Chiricahua Apaches and the USA can be seen as the conflict between the differing conception of warfare of a mechanical society and an organic society. In the short term, the close ties and warrior culture combined with an adept approach to guerrilla warfare gave huge tactical advantages to the Apaches. However, in the long term, an organic society such as the USA could simply divert a fraction of its resources to this conflict and still wear the Apaches down.

For example, the Chiricahua Apaches killed 28 men from the 9th Cavalry between May 1879 and August 1881. This appears to be a small number, yet between 1866 and 1890 that regiment lost a total of 44 men killed in action.

The grave of a 6th Cavalry soldier, one of two men who had just deserted from their regiment and were ambushed by Apaches led by Nana in March 1880. Both men were killed but, according to the Apache scouts who found their bodies, they both had put up a courageous fight. Theirs was the fate of many individuals who underestimated the risks of traveling through Apacheria. The fact that one can simply stumble across such graves today gives a very tangible link to events of the past. (Author's photo)

In other words, in less than three years Chiricahua Apaches with Mescalero Apache allies inflicted 64 per cent of the regiment's total fatalities in the first 24 years of its history. Between September 4 and 30, 1879, Chiricahua Apaches killed ten men from the 9th Cavalry, so in the space of four weeks they inflicted 23 per cent of the fatalities sustained between 1866 and 1890. However, while the Chiricahua Apache warriors could clearly inflict physical and psychological damage far in excess of what could be expected of their small numbers, they simply could not inflict enough damage on the USA to deter its expansion into the Southwest. It is a testament to their ability as guerrillas that it took the USA almost 30 years to break their resistance.

 AFTER THE BATTLE – CHIVALO WATERHOLES, NOVEMBER 1880

About one month after Victorio was killed at Tres Castillos on October 14/15, 1880, a nine-man Chihuahua state cavalry patrol was wiped out by survivors of Victorio's band. Some of Victorio's possessions and his saddle were recovered from one of the soldiers. The furious Apaches then hacked the man's body into bits. This was an extremely unusual action for Apaches. One Apache recalled many years later that while they did not fear death they did fear the dead and so they minimized their contact with dead bodies. It was for this reason that the Apaches rarely scalped and usually only did so in retaliation for the scalping of their own people by their enemies. They never retained scalps as trophies. In this case, one suspects that this was an extreme reaction to the loss of their leader. There is no clear account of how Victorio was killed at Tres Castillos and the Apaches clearly state that he committed suicide rather than be taken alive. The Mexican soldier may have killed Victorio and taken the possessions or taken them from his body; either way this would have outraged these Apaches.

After battle, it was standard practice for the Chiricahua Apaches to make sure that the enemy was dead. They either used rocks or rifle butts to the head and/or lances to stab the body. Reports of Apache attacks often talk about lurid mutilations. However, these were mainly the warriors making sure that their enemies were not capable of suddenly rising up and taking them by surprise.

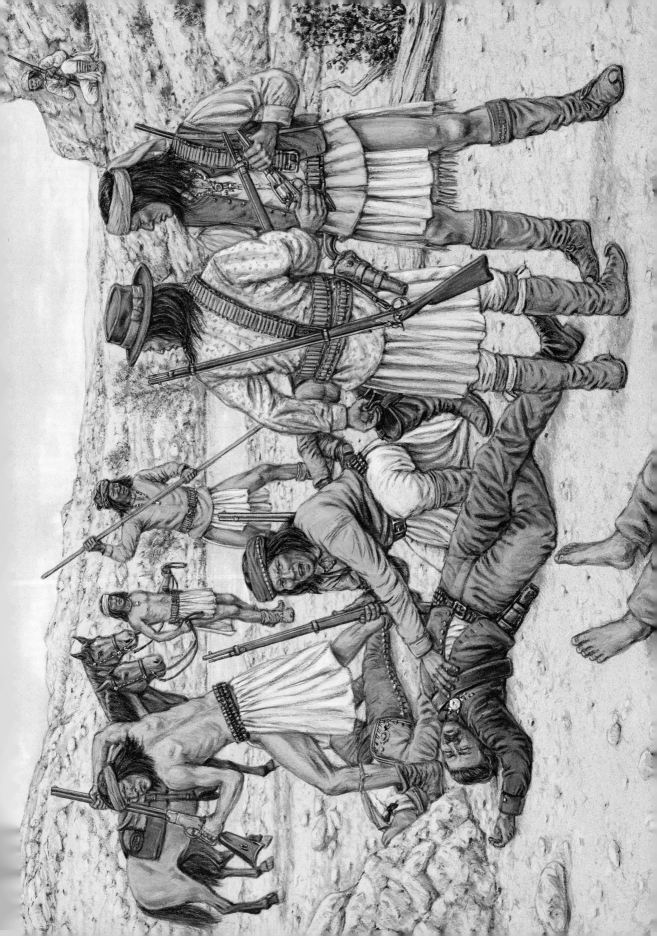

FURTHER READING

The two key books on understanding Apache warriors and society are:

Opler, M. E., *An Apache Life-Way: The Economic, Social, & Religious Institutions of the Chiricahua Indians*, University of Nebraska Press, Lincoln (1996). First published by University of Chicago Press in 1941.

Goodwin, G., *Western Apache Raiding and Warfare*, University of Arizona Press, Tuscon (1998)

The following article gives an excellent overview of the apprenticeship of a Chiricahua warrior:

Opler, M. E. & Hoijer, H., 'The Raid and War-Path Language of the Chiricahua Apache,' in *American Anthropologist* Vol. XLII, (Oct–Dec 1940), pp.617–34.

There was an online version of this article at: http://www.jstor.org/stable/663656 as of 15 August 2013.

Below is listed some of the more easily accessible and available material which gives a good introduction to the Apaches and the Apache Wars.

Ball, E., *In the Days of Victorio: Recollections of a Warm Springs Apache*, University of Arizona Press, Tucson (1970)

Ball, E., with Henn N. &. Sánchez, L. A., *Indeh: An Apache Odyssey*, University of Oklahoma Press, Norman (1980)

Betzinez, J., *I Fought with Geronimo*, University of Nebraska Press, London (1987). First published by Stackpole in 1959.

Cozzens, P., *Eyewitnesses to the Indian Wars 1865–1890 Volume 1: The Struggle for Apacheria*, Stackpole Books, Mechanicsville (2001)

Cruse, T., *Apache Days and After*, University of Nebraska Press, London (1987). First published by The Caxton Printers Ltd in 1941.

Eggan, F. (Ed), *Social Anthropology of North American Tribes*, University of Chicago Press, Chicago (1955)

Haley, J. L., *Apaches: A History and Culture Portrait*, University of Oklahoma Press, Norman (1981)

Hook, J., *The Apaches*, Osprey Publishing, London (1987)

Laumbach, K. W., *Hembrillo, An Apache Battlefield of the Victorio War: The Archaeology and History of the Hembrillo Battlefield*, Prepared for the White Sands Missile Range, New Mexico by Human Systems Research Inc. (2001)

Laumbach, K. W., Scott, D. D. & Wakeman, J., *Conline's Skirmish: An Episode of the Victorio War. Archaeological and Historical Documentation of an 1880s Skirmish Site on White Sands Missile Range.* Prepared for the Directorate of Public Works, White Sands Missile Range, New Mexico by Human Systems Research Inc. (2005)

Roberts, D., *Once They Moved Like The Wind: Cochise, Geronimo and the Apache Wars*, Pimlico, London (1998)

Robinson, S., *Apache Voices: Their Stories of Survival as Told to Eve Ball*, University of New Mexico Press, Albuquerque (2000)

Shapard, B., *Chief Loco: Apache Peacemaker*, University of Oklahoma Press, Norman (2010)

Sweeney, E. R., *Cochise: Chiricahua Apache Chief*, University of Oklahoma Press, Norman (1991)

Sweeney, E. R., *Mangas Coloradas: Chief of the Chiricahua Apaches*, University of Oklahoma Press, Norman (1998)

Sweeney, E. R., *From Cochise to Geronimo: The Chiricahua Apaches 1874–1886*, University of Oklahoma Press, Norman (2010)

Thrapp, D. L., *The Conquest of Apacheria*, University of Oklahoma Press, London (1967)

Thrapp, D. L., *Victorio and the Mimbres Apaches*, University of Oklahoma Press, London (1974)

Wood, L., *Chasing Geronimo: The Journal of Leonard Wood May – September, 1886*, University of New Mexico Press, Albuquerque (1970). Edited & Introduced by Jack C. Lane

Worcester, D. E., *The Apaches: Eagles of the Southwest*, University of Oklahoma Press, Norman (1979)

INDEX

References to images and illustrations are in bold; captions to illustrations are in brackets.